Newhaven Fort and Garrison

Newhaven Fort and Garrison

Newhaven Fort and Newhaven Garrison during the Great War 1914–1918

Keith Brain

Reveille Press is an imprint of
Tommies Guides Military Booksellers & Publishers

Gemini House
136–140 Old Shoreham Road
Brighton
BN3 7BD

www.tommiesguides.co.uk

First published in Great Britain by
Reveille Press 2014

For more information please visit
www.reveillepress.com

A catalogue record for this book is available
from the British Library

ISBN 978-1-908336-32-3

Cover design by Reveille Press
Typeset by Vivian@Bookscribe

Printed and bound in Great Britain

KEITH BRAIN is a volunteer researcher with Newhaven Fort, Fort Rise, Newhaven, East Sussex, BN9 9DS, telephone number 01273 517622, www.newhavenfort.org.uk.

Over 15 years ago his interest in the Great War was stimulated by his research into the service of his grandfathers and great-uncles in the Great War. He has also carried out research for the Soldiers of Oxfordshire museum in the county of his birth.

In 2012 he produced the book *The Life and Death of a Royal Field Artillery Subaltern on the Western Front*, published by Reveille Press, from information sources in the Newhaven Fort Archive.

He retired in March 2008 and lives in Newhaven. He is a member of the Western Front Association (W.F.A.) and the Sussex Military History Society.

PREFACE

The primary objectives for producing this book were to identify the men, as far as possible, and their units that served in Newhaven Fort during the Great War and to describe the activities at the Fort.

During research, however, it was soon found that the Fort was an integral part of the Newhaven Garrison during the war with thousands of servicemen from various units billeted in and around Newhaven Town as well as in the Fort itself. It was necessary, therefore, to extend the scope of the book to identify and provide details about the other units and the activities of the Newhaven Garrison to best describe the role that Newhaven Fort played in the war, especially as part of the Garrison. Whilst some garrison details were found to be not directly connected to the Fort it was considered to be of such interest that it should be included.

The author wishes to make clear, however, that the information about the other units in the Garrison, though informative, is not intended to be exhaustive.

The research then revealed the answers to some intriguing questions. Newhaven Fort, town and harbour were never attacked/invaded during the war. What if Newhaven had been subjected to a hostile attack or invasion? What kinds of attack were expected? How and by whom would any hostile attack have been repulsed? The answers to these questions may be found in this book.

LIST OF ILLUSTRATIONS

		Page No.
1.	A Newhaven Fort 6 inch gun with Seaford Bay in the background	Front Cover/ Title page
2.	Map of Garrison Area	16,17
3.	Newhaven Fort from the River Ouse	26
4.	Aerial View of Newhaven Bridge looking East 1916	26
5.	Manning a Newhaven Fort 6 ins gun	41
6.	Sussex Royal Garrison Artillery N.C.O. s September 1914	41
7.	The tug "Alert" towing the brigantine "Sussex Maid" circa 1912	42
8.	Lighthouse at the end of the breakwater, Newhaven Harbour	42
9.	Searchlight emplacement, West Beach – demolished in the 1960s	43
10.	Group of Sussex R.G.A men on parade ground of the camouflaged Fort	43
11.	1915 Christmas card sent by Sussex R.G.A. officers	44
12.	Sussex Fortress Company R.E. Newhaven – Working Party	52
13.	Christmas and New Year card sent by 2/1 Sussex (Fortress) R.E., Newhaven	52
14.	Plan View of Newhaven Fort 1914	56
15.	Badge of the London Electrical Engineers March 1916	57
16.	London Electrical Engineers postcard	58
17.	578 Works Company, Sussex Fortress Engineers June 1917	60
18.	C.S.M. Wells leading 578 Works Company through Bridge Street, Newhaven	62
19.	Brigadier General Frederick Gore Anley C.B., C.M.G.	64
20.	Newhaven Special Military Area Public Notice regarding entry 1st March 1917	65
21.	Defence of the Realm Public Notice on Sale of Pistols 9th March 1917	66
22.	Major J.T. Chapman, Royal Artillery, C.O. No. 1 Depot, R.G.A.	69

		Page No.
23.	Major S.W.P. Beale, 4th Battalion Royal Sussex Regiment	95
24.	4th Battalion, Royal Sussex Regiment on parade prior to leaving Newhaven April 1916	95
25.	Postcard to Private Harold Carver from his wife - 'Loneliness' August 1916	102
26.	Newhaven Garrison Troops on Parade on Newhaven Recreation Ground	103
27.	Second Lieutenant J. B. Lane – Training Course Report 23rd August 1915	108
28.	Second Lieutenant J. B. Lane – O.C. Training Certificate 23rd August 1915	109
29.	Second Lieutenant J. B. Lane – Solicitor's Letter 26th November 1915	110–112
30.	Permit Book of Bertrand Russell December 1916	115
31.	Newhaven Fortress News Front Page 20th November 1914	119
32.	Newhaven Fortress News Editorial Page 20th November 1914	120
33.	Cartoon of 'Submarine Section' London Electrical Engineers	122
34.	Cartoon "Christmas On Outpost Duty"	127
35.	Medal Index Card for Private Thomas Bartram	137
36.	Grave headstone of Private Thomas Bartram, Newhaven Cemetery.	137
37.	Medal Index Card for Private Elias Luff	139
38.	Copy of Statement of Captain Price R.F.A. regarding Private A.B. Saunders	144–145
39.	Newhaven Garrison Strength Return 13th April 1917	171
40.	Newspaper report of Sussex (Fortress) Royal Engineers New Years dinner 7th January 1916	172–175
41.	Poem 'King George's Boys at Newhaven 1914'	181
42.	Fort Armament in the Great War	182
43.	Letter to David Lloyd George February 1920	183
44.	Fort Site Plan 2013	184

CONTENTS

Preface.....7
List of Illustrations.....8
Introduction to Newhaven Fort.....12
Objectives of a Newhaven Garrison.....15
Newhaven War Garrison Accommodation Plans – 12 Feb 1913.....18
Outbreak of War 4th August 1914.....20
Newhaven Garrison Defence – Available Forces and their
Defensive Duties.....21
Authorised Troops.....21
Additional Troops.....22
Naval Forces.....23
Air Forces.....23
Assistance from Outside.....23
Newhaven Fort and Garrison Establishments and Armaments 1914-1918.....24
Sussex R.G.A. in Newhaven Fort.....27
Fort Commanding Officers 1914-1918.....45
50 Anti-Aircraft Company R.G.A. Newhaven Fort.....48
Fortress Company, Royal Engineers, Territorial Force – Fort Hill Camp.....50
4 Company London Electrical Engineers R.E. T.F. in Newhaven Fort.....53
Signals R.E. T.F. in Newhaven Fort.....59
578 Works Company, Sussex Fortress Engineers, R.E. Fort Hill Camp.....60
The Newhaven Garrison.....63
Garrison Commanders.....63
No. 1 Depot R.G.A. – From 5th August 1914 to 16th May 1915.....67
Royal Defence Corps......70
12th & 13th (Transport Workers) Battalions, Bedfordshire Regiment.....72
29th (Works) Battalion, Middlesex Regiment.....73
53rd Anti-Aircraft Company R.E.....74
4th Battalion T.F., Royal Sussex Regiment from 5th August 1914
to 24th April 1915.....75
3rd (Reserve) Battalion, Royal Sussex Regiment from
16th May 1915 to the end of the war.....96

Royal Army Medical Corps (R.A.M.C.) 116
'Newhaven Fortress News' 118
Soldier Fatalities in Newhaven 128
Private Herbert Charles Jay 10754, 3rd Battalion, Royal Sussex Regiment, 28th May 1915 128
Private Thomas Bartram, GSSR/67, No. 8 Company, 3rd Battalion, Royal Sussex Regiment, 6th Dec 1915 129
Lance Corporal Elias Luff, L/4705, 3rd Battalion, Royal Sussex Regiment, attached to Newhaven Garrison Military Police 18th April 1916 138
Private Cecil Clifton, 5124, 3rd Battalion, Royal Sussex Regiment, 20th April 1916 139
Lance Corporal Arthur Thomas Twine, G/5639, 3rd Battalion, Royal Sussex Regiment, 16th Jan 1917 140
Private Allen Bernard Sanders, 19561, 3rd Battalion, Royal Sussex Regiment, 24th Jan 1917 143
Newhaven Port Statistics 147

Appendix 148
1. Abbreviations/Glossary of Terms 148
2. Bibliography 150
3. "Newhaven Defence Scheme (Provisional) Revised to April 1918" ... 152
4. Daily Strength Return Newhaven Garrison 13th April 1917 171
5. Newspaper report on Sussex (Fortress) R.E. Annual Dinner 7th Jan 1916 172
6. Cartoon and Poem - 'King George's Boys at Newhaven 1914' 181
7. The Armament in the Fort in the Great War 182
8. Letter to David Lloyd George February 1920 183
9. Newhaven Fort Site Plan 2014 184
10. Acknowledgements 185

INTRODUCTION TO NEWHAVEN FORT

Seaford Bay and the port of Newhaven were always tempting landing places for an invader and the defensive history of the area dates back to the Bronze Age when a large enclosed fort was built on the cliff top. When the Romans arrived, they too built a fort on the site and, since that time fortifications have remained, culminating in the building of the Newhaven Fort structure seen today.

Newhaven Fort was built around the 1860's and is the largest work of defence ever constructed in Sussex. Pre-1914 the troops at Newhaven Fort were regular soldiers of the Royal Garrison Artillery, but Newhaven Fort was also used to train volunteers – part-time soldiers who became known as Territorials in 1908.

By 1914, a considerable amount of modernisation had taken place at the Fort. The old style muzzle-loading guns were replaced by up-to-date breech-loading types with a much higher rate of fire and the gun positions altered or rebuilt to suit the new weapons. The soldiers' living quarters had been improved; four baths had been added and a 'recreation room' was established

When the Great War started in August 1914, the Territorials of the Sussex Royal Garrison Artillery took over the manning of Newhaven Fort from the peacetime garrison regulars, No. 1 Depot, R.G.A. (Royal Garrison Artillery). In addition to the gunners of the Sussex RGA, there were Sussex Fortress Royal Engineers (T.F.) and London Electrical Royal Engineers (T.F.) manning searchlights out on the harbour breakwater and an infantry battalion the Special Service section, 4th Battalion, Royal Sussex Regiment.

During the First World War Newhaven became a major military supply port for the British Expeditionary Force in France. The total tonnage during the war amounted to over six million tons. It was also a base for naval vessels on escort and other duties in the English Channel. Hospital ships brought back wounded soldiers from France. On the East side of the mouth of the River Ouse at Tidemills a seaplane base operated aircraft on anti-submarine patrols from 1917.

With this degree of military importance, the area was well defended. The

Fort's two 6in guns were manned to work in association with a naval examination vessel, operating in the vicinity of the harbour mouth. This vessel's responsibility was to challenge and inspect all shipping approaching the harbour. If its order to stop was ignored, a Fort gun would put a shot across the bows of the offender.

Although an assault on the port of Newhaven was always considered as a military possibility, it never became a reality. With heavy casualties on the Western Front, fit men were posted away from the Fort to more active service.

When the Great War ended, the garrison consisted largely of troops in low medical grades. With peacetime, Newhaven Fort became almost deserted. A Master Gunner with one NCO and a couple of civilian labourers were required only to keep the place in good order and service the guns.

The Fort was again called upon to play its part with the outbreak of the Second World War, but that is another story.

Newhaven Fort has stood firm as a vital element in Britain's coastal defence through two World Wars. Following its abandonment as a military fortification in the 1960's it suffered years of incredible neglect and dereliction but has now been restored to provide an award-winning visitor attraction.

Today it attracts many visitors and a 2014 site plan can be seen in the Appendix illustrating the current layout and attractions.

OBJECTIVES OF A NEWHAVEN GARRISON

A Garrison at Newhaven was necessary for the:

a) Defence of Newhaven Fort against hostile attack from the sea or land.
b) Defence within the limits of the Garrison Area against enemy landing forces with objectives beyond the Garrison.
c) Support of the Examination Service, the floating portion of which was under the Royal Navy.
d) Protection of vulnerable points against acts of sabotage.

The area of the Garrison was bounded by the Coast Line from Friars Bay (what is now Peacehaven) on the West to Blatchington Coast Guard Station on the East, and roughly by a circle of 1 ½ miles radius, having its centre at Newhaven Town Station.

The perceived objectives of a hostile attack were to destroy the quays, shipping, ammunition and stores. A possible, though improbable object was thought to be to secure the harbour and beach for landing an invading force.

The forms of attack considered likely and provided for were:

a) Bombardment at night by enemy submarines.
b) A small landing party at night from enemy submarines.

Improbable forms of attack were considered to be:

a) A landing of considerable force preceded by a bombardment from the sea with the battery in the Fort as its objective.
b) An attack from the land by force which had already landed in the vicinity.

Full details of the defensive actions to be employed in the event of such attacks can be found in the copy of the document "Newhaven Defence Scheme (Provisional) Revised to April 1918" in the Appendix.

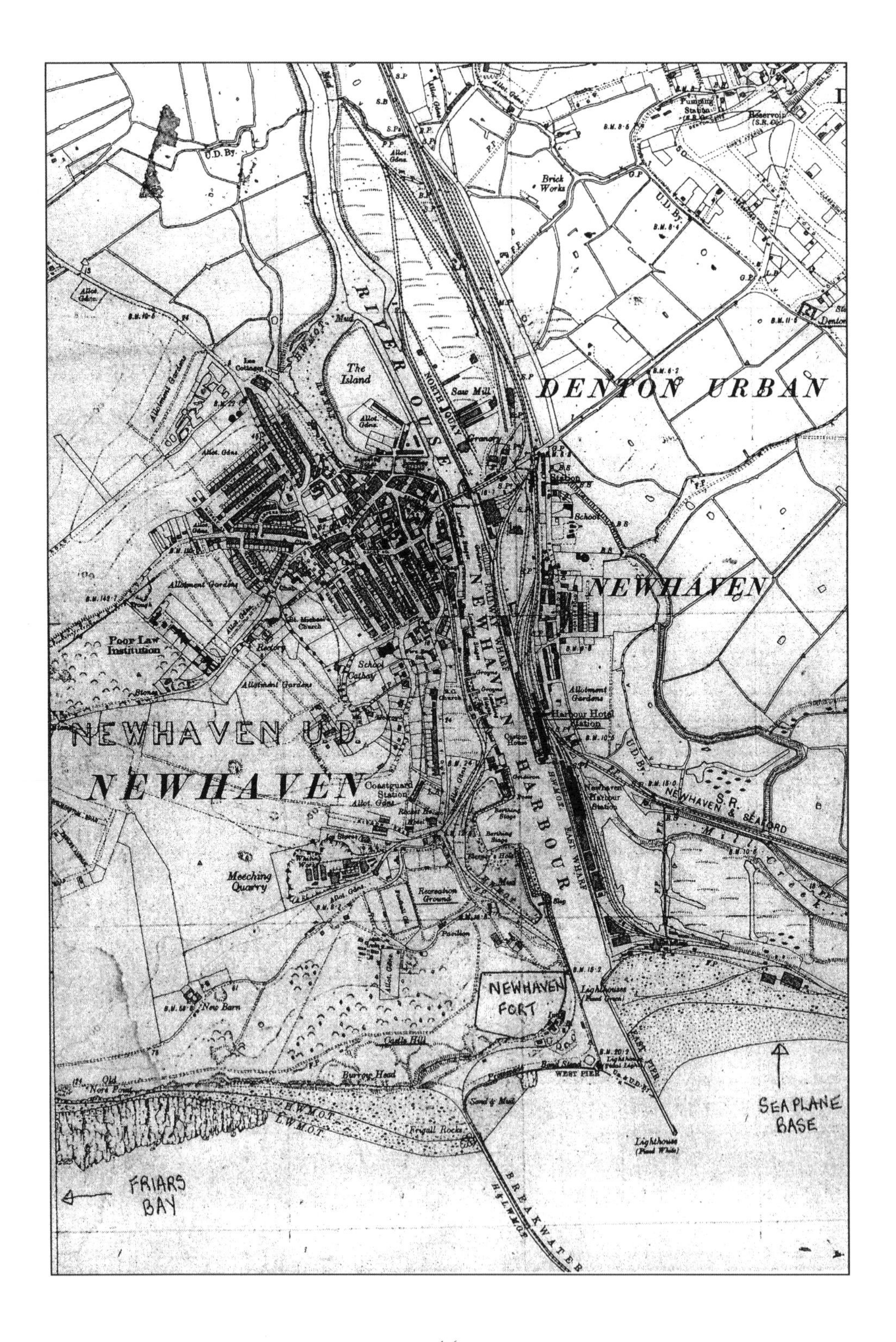
DENTON URBAN
NEWHAVEN
RIVER OUSE
NORTH QUAY
The Island
Saw Mill
Granary
Brick Works
Station
School
Poor Law Institution
Allotment Gardens
NEWHAVEN U.D.
NEWHAVEN
NEWHAVEN HARBOUR
Harbour Hotel
Coastguard Station
Meeching Quarry
Recreation Ground
Pavilion
EAST WHARF
Newhaven Harbour Station
NEWHAVEN & SEAFORD
NEWHAVEN FORT
Castle Hill
Burrow Head
WEST PIER
EAST PIER
Lighthouse
BREAKWATER
SEAPLANE BASE
FRIARS BAY

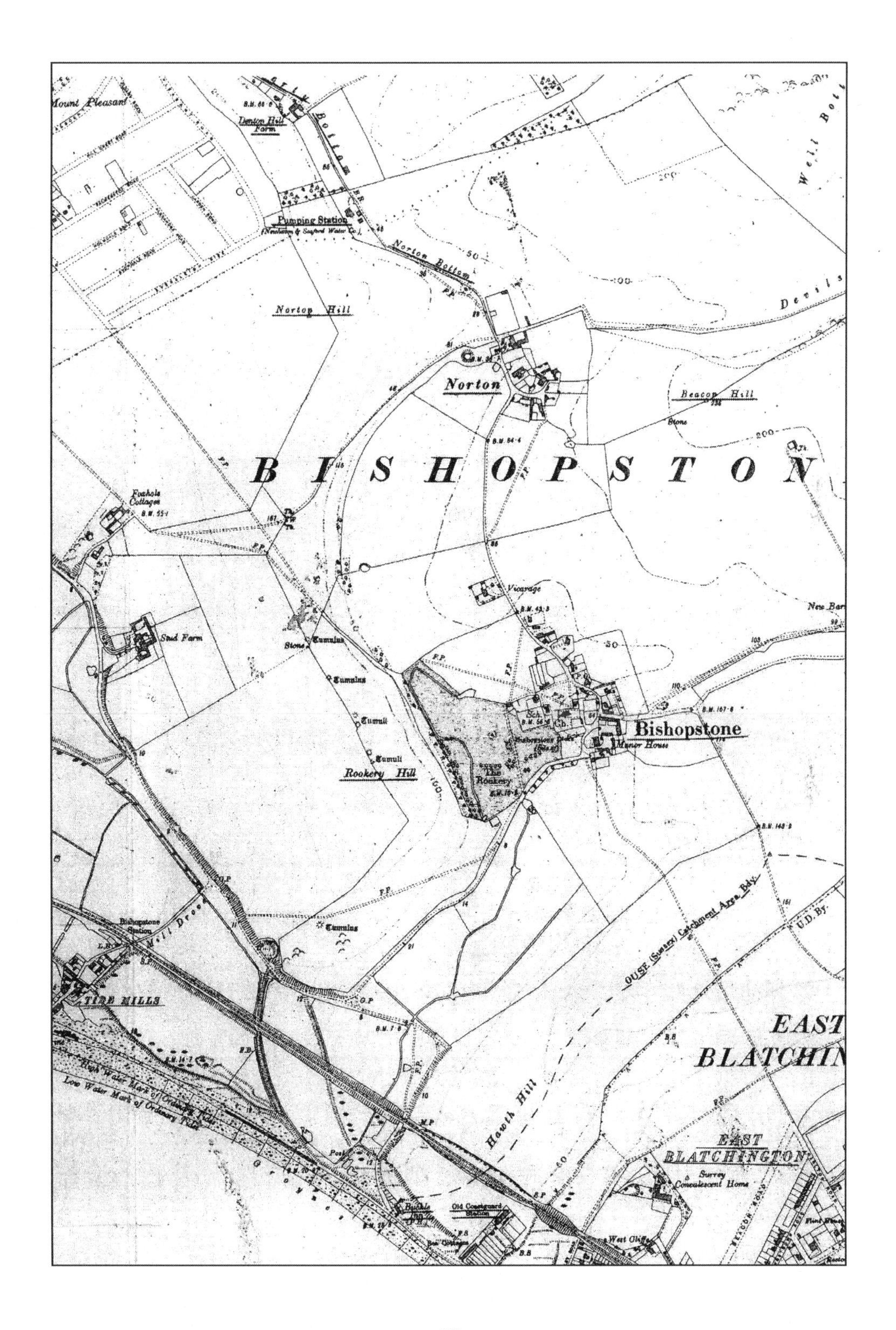
Mount Pleasant
Denton Hill Farm
Pumping Station
(Newhaven & Seaford Water Co.)
Norton Bottom
Norton Hill
Norton
Beacon Hill
Stone
Devils
BISHOPSTON
Foxhole Cottages
Vicarage
New Bar
Stud Farm
Stone
Tumulus
Tumulus
Tumuli
Tumuli
Rookery Hill
The Rookery
Sch.
Ch.
Bishopstone
Manor House
Bishopstone Station
TIDE MILLS
High Water Mark of Ordinary Tides
Low Water Mark of Ordinary Tides
Tumulus
OUSE (Sussex) Catchment Area Bdy.
U.D. By.
EAST BLATCHIN
Hawth Hill
EAST BLATCHINGTON
Surrey Convalescent Home
Old Coastguard Station
West Cliff

NEWHAVEN WAR GARRISON
ACCOMMODATION PLANS
12 FEBRUARY 1913

The strategic importance of the port of Newhaven necessitated forward planning of the accommodation of defensive units in the event of a war. A Garrison accommodation plan for such a defence was produced in February 1913, 17 months before the outbreak of the Great War.

The plan was stamped with '**South Eastern Coast Defences Dover**' and the date '**12th Feb 1913**'. It was inscribed '***O.C. Det. R.G.A S.E.C.D, Newhaven. For Information***' and signed by **Major Wadington, General Staff, South Eastern Coast Defences** and contained the following details:

ACCOMMODATION OF NEWHAVEN WAR GARRISON

Unit	**Officers**	**O.R.s**	**How Accommodated**	**Remarks**
Headquarters	2	4	The Fort	
Details R.G.A	1	37	The Fort	Includes 33 Other Ranks from Dover
Sussex R.G.A (1 Coy.)	7	121	The Fort	Includes Per. Staff.
3rd (F) Coy. R.E.	1	7	The Fort	From Dover
Sussex (F) R.E.	3	98	Drill Hall (78), Marshall Hall (20) Bridge Hotel (3 Officers)	Includes Per. Staff.
London Electrical Engineers	2	27	The Fort	

Note: No. 1 Company Sussex R.G.A. at this time was based in Brighton.

4th Btn. Royal Sussex Regt.	Officers	O.R.s	How Accommodated	Remarks
1 Company	3	117	The Fort	Total of 30 Officers, 984 O.R.s i.e. War Establishment less 6 drivers A.S.C. for 2nd Line Transport
1 Company	3	117	Engineers House, Norton Bottom (3 Officers) Denton Hill Farm & Norton Farm, Norton Bottom (117 O.R.s)	
1 Company	3	117	Meeching Farm	
1 Company	3	117	Old Isolation Hospital, Beaty's Barn & Workhouse	
Remainder of Battalion		70	Lodging House, River Walk	
	18	37	Liberal Club	
		*90	Drill Hall, Meeching Road	* now being converted into private rooms, gymnasium is available, also Salvation Army Hostel
		75	Cinema, High Street	
		30	Cinema, Chapel Street	
		214	Disused Brewery	
Details A.S.C.	2	12	The Fort	
Details R.A.M.C.	5	15	3 Officers (Civil Practitioners) – private accommodation 2 Officers & 15 O.R.s at The Fort	

OUTBREAK OF WAR 4TH AUGUST 1914

Newhaven passed under naval and military control immediately following the outbreak of hostilities. The Harbour Railway Station was closed to the public forthwith, the only trains allowed to stop there being those that did so to set down or pick up military authorities.On and from 22nd September 1916, the town of Newhaven and all the land within the limits of the military defences became a special military area under the Defence of the Realm Regulations, and no passengers arriving at Newhaven Town Station were allowed to leave it unless they held a permit issued by the Commandant of the area. Newhaven was thus given up to the handling of Government traffic for the duration of the war. [These conditions were in force until 2nd December 1918, when the restriction was suspended 'until further notice'.]

A bank of sidings principally for stabling ammunition trains was laid out on the down side, north of Newhaven Town Station. Grenades were made at the South Heighton Cement Works and brought out of the works by the Harbour 'Terrier' locomotive. [During 1918 trains were arriving every ½ hour.]

The Port of Newhaven then commenced its duties as a Home Base for the Shipment of ammunition and supplies to the British Expeditionary Force, repatriation of wounded soldiers from France, a base for Naval Forces employed on escort duty for Government Transports and on mine sweeping and anti-submarine patrol duties.

Having been at the Fort since 1908, on 5th August 1914 No. 1 Depot, Royal Garrison Artillery vacated the Fort and was accommodated in the Council Schools and public buildings in Newhaven. The Fort was taken over by the Sussex R.G.A. (T.F) and Fortress Company, Royal Engineers. The 4th Battalion, Royal Sussex Regiment also arrived on 5th August 1914 and some of the men were accommodated in the Fort, but the majority of them were encamped a short distance away at Meeching Rise.

NEWHAVEN GARRISON DEFENCE

AVAILABLE FORCES AND THEIR DEFENSIVE DUTIES

AUTHORISED TROOPS

The troops authorised for the defence of the garrison consisted of:
1 Special Reserve infantry battalion
1 Company R.G.A. (T.F.)
1 Fortress Company R.E. (Electric Lights and Signals)
1 Works Company R.E. (T.F.)

SUSSEX R.G.A.

This was No. 1 Company initially and No. 2 Company was formed later. The Company manned the fixed Coast Defence Armament in the Fort and also undertook the immediate defence of the Fort. The Battery Commander was further responsible for the tactical handling of defences of the Breakwater and Foreshore below the Fort.

FORTRESS COMPANY R.E.

The Fortress Company, R.E. (Electric Light Section) manned the Defence Electric Lights under the tactical control of the Battery Commander. The searchlights on the BREAKWATER were permanently manned and ready for action. The Signal Section was responsible for telephone communications and despatch riders.

SPECIAL RESERVE INFANTRY BATTALION

This was the 4th Battalion, Royal Sussex Regiment until 24th April 1915 when it was posted away and replaced by 3rd (Special Reserve) Battalion, Royal Sussex Regiment.

The regiment was responsible for the first line of defence on the foreshore in both Eastern and Western Sections. For this purpose it maintained a Guard of 2 N.C.O. s and 6 men in the BREAKWATER AREA by day and night, two Maxim Gun detachments in the FORT by night, ready to take post in the in the BREAKWATER AREA at short notice, and a Piquet of 1 Officer and 20 Other Ranks near the NAVAL WIRELESS STATION in the Eastern Section.

(In times of Special Vigilance the Maxim Gun detachments and the Piquet would remain at their posts by day and night, and the Piquet would be reinforced by 1 Lewis Gun and detachment and by 16 other ranks to provide two Sentry groups at TIDE MILLS and near the BUCKLE INN respectively, and a Patrol between these points)

The bulk of the Battalion acted as the General Reserve under the Garrison Commander.

A Coast Watching outpost at CHALK GAP near FRIARS BAY would be furnished on emergency.

WORKS COMPANY R.E.

The Works Company R.E. was held in reserve for any R.E. Services that the situation may have required.

ADDITIONAL TROOPS

In addition, the following troops were available to be used though not permanently authorised for the Defence of the Garrison:

ROYAL DEFENCE CORPS

The Royal Defence Corps furnished permanent guards on the entrance to the Newhaven Prohibited Area.

TRANSPORT WORKERS

The Detachments of the 12th and 13th Transport Workers Battalion of the Bedfordshire Regiment were employed on transport work in the harbour. They would, so long as rifles were available, and work on the quays had been suspended, be responsible in an emergency, for the second line of defence in the Eastern Section. This extended from the South end of the EAST WHARF to the salient in the existing trenches of the Eastern Defences, immediately north of the London, Brighton & South Coast Railway (L.B. & S.C.R.) (Newhaven and Seaford Branch).

The Detachment would also form a local Reserve in the Eastern Section under the Garrison Commander. Half of this Reserve would be used by the O.C., Detachment, (who would act as Commander, Eastern Section, in emergency) at his discretion.

A Guard on the L.B. & S.C.R. Pumping Station and Reservoir at DENTON would also be furnished.

300 Stands of Arms (1914 pattern rifles), 50 rounds of S.A.A. [small arms ammunition] per rifle in bandoliers, and 50 rounds per rifle in boxes, on the charge of the 3rd Royal Sussex Regiment, were kept in the RAILWAY ROAD CAMP, for issue to the Detachment on the alarm being given.

NAVAL FORCES

A variable number of Naval Ratings were present in the Port on board Torpedo Boats, Mine Sweepers, Drifters and Patrol Boats, and assistance could have been rendered, if possible under the orders of the Senior Naval Officer, but no reliance could be placed on those forces as they would possibly have been employed at sea when the emergency arose. Reliance was placed upon the Naval Authorities for Intelligence of the approach of hostile Submarines or other Vessels, which would be obtained from patrols or from a system of hydrophones which existed in the vicinity of the Port connected with a station at Cuckmere Haven.

The daily naval activities were at the Port War Signal Station which watched all approaches from the sea and the Hydrophone Circle which was manned to watch for the approach of submarines. In addition at night or in thick fog a line of trawlers were anchored ½ mile off shore, except in rough weather.

AIR FORCES

The personnel of the Air Station on Tidemills, created 1917, were also at times available with two Lewis Guns, unless otherwise engaged in its submarine and mine patrol duties.

ASSISTANCE FROM OUTSIDE

The only troops located in the neighbourhood of the Garrison were the Canadian Training Centre at Seaford, and assistance in considerable force could be available provided other schemes for their movement elsewhere were not in force.
[At various times throughout the war other units were based in Seaford]

NEWHAVEN FORT AND GARRISON

ESTABLISHMENTS AND ARMAMENTS 1914-1918

Establishments varied throughout the war. The figures below are from the Newhaven Defence Plan Revised to 1918 (see appendix):

2 Company, Sussex R.G.A., (T.F.) in the Fort

Establishment – 4 Officers, 86 Other Ranks
Guns – 2, 6 inch B.L. Mark VII
Ammunition – 525 rounds per gun
Rifles – 86 1914 [1914 Pattern Rifle P14, Lee-Enfield, 5 round magazine]
Ammunition – 550 Rounds Equipment; 200 Rounds Reserve per rifle

3rd (Reserve) Battalion, Royal Sussex Regiment at Meeching Rise Camp

Rifles - 500 S.M.L.E. [Short Magazine Lee-Enfield] for Drafts,
730 1914 Pattern,
365 MLE [Magazine Lee-Enfield, .303 calibre],
365 EY [Ernest Youlle, the inventor. It was an adaptation of the Lee-Enfield rifle] or D.P. [Drill Purpose rifles. This was a rifle that had been altered so that it could no longer be fired. It was used for rifle drill and weapon- handling tests].
Ammunition - 550 Rounds Equipment, 200 Rounds Reserve per Rifle.
Machine Guns – 2 Maxims [A four man crew was required to man each Maxim]. Located in the Fort.
Ammunition – 10,000 Rounds Equipment, 21,500 Rounds Reserve per Machine Gun.

Fortress Company R.E.

London Electrical Engineers R.E. (T.F.) and Signals Company R.E. in the Fort

Establishment – 3 Officers, 58 Other Ranks

Lights – 2 x 90 cm. Projectors Clarke Chapman Lamps

Rifles – 6 E.Y. Ammunition - 550 Rounds Equipment, 200 Rounds Reserve per rifle

578th Works Company, R.E. at Fort Hill Camp

Establishment – 3 Officers, 147 men

Rifles – 18 MLE Ammunition - 550 Rounds Equipment, 200 Rounds Reserve per rifle

The fighting strength for these units (excluding 3rd (Reserve) Battalion, Royal Sussex) was kept up to Establishment.

On 18th April 1918 the establishment and its breakdown in the Fort was given as follows:

1 Fire (Fort) Commander – Lieutenant-Colonel
1 Adjutant – Captain (acted as Fort Commander's assistant)
1 Instructor in Gunnery – Subaltern (Junior Officer e.g. Second Lieutenant)
1 Battery Commander – Captain
4 G.G.C. s. - Subalterns (Junior Officers e.g. Second Lieutenants)
1 Master Gunner – Warrant Officer
1 Battery Sergeant-Major – Warrant Officer
1 Battery Quarter-Master Sergeant – Staff Sergeant
3 Artificers – 1x L/Sergeant, 2 x Gunners
2 Trumpeters – Gunners
95 Manning & Administrative Detail - 3 x Staff Sergeants/Sergeants
7 x Lance Sergeants
7 x Bombardiers
7 x Lance Bombardiers
71 x Gunners.

TOTALS: 8 Officers 103 Other Ranks = 111

Newhaven Fort during the war – from the River Ouse [NFA]

Aerial View of Newhaven Bridge looking East – 1916 with Railway Road Camp in the background. [NHM]

SUSSEX R.G.A. IN NEWHAVEN FORT

The main occupier of the Fort, Sussex Royal Garrison Artillery, did not maintain a war diary during the Great War, a common occurrence for UK based Territorial Force units. The primary source of information about the Sussex R.G.A in the Fort is the memoirs of men who served in the Fort during the war. They give an invaluable insight into the occupiers and their activities in the Fort during this period.

The Sussex R.G.A. Company (T.F.) was based in Brighton and in July 1914 it was ordered to attend annual training camp at Newhaven.

> 'It was decided that we should march from Brighton to Newhaven with full equipment, accompanied by the R.A.M.C. T.A. and R.A.S.C. T.A. who were also in the Gloucester Road drill hall and a horse drawn ambulance and wagon with our kit. The regular Royal Garrison Artillery were in occupation of the Fort at Newhaven with married quarters in Gibbons [Gibbon] Road and the Trumpet Band of the Depot under Trumpet Major Lyons met us the top of town and with much Gusto and blaring of bands we marched into camp. We carried out 6 ins gun practice until the 3rd August at the Fort and on Monday 4th August was a Bank Holiday Monday [Monday was actually 3rd August, not the 4th] and a day when wives were to visit their men in camp, but on Sunday evening we were told not to turn in but get kitted up to move off and at midnight we were ordered to fall in and quietly we marched down Money Bag Hill past the Sheffield Hotel along Fort Road and up Fort Hill. As we came abreast of the gymnasium No. 1 Deport, R.G.A. passed us on the way to pick up their guns and batteries for them to join the B.E.F. and with a quiet "Eyes Right" we saluted each other and we took over the Fort, which I understand is named 'GLACIS' which means apparently 'on a hill' with myself as a Boy Trumpeter and my father [Charles George Cornford] as Battery Sergeant Major.'
>
> Corporal C.E. Cornford R.G.A

NOTES:

1. There are date discrepancies in his account but it would appear that the Sussex R.G.A. actually moved into the Fort on Monday 3rd August before war was declared on Tuesday the 4th August. However No. 1 Depot R.G.A. records state that it vacated the Fort on 5th August 1914, a Thursday.
2. A glacis in military engineering is an artificial slope of earth used in late European fortresses so constructed as to keep any potential assailant under the fire of the defenders until the last possible moment.

The following day, 3rd August 1914, was a Bank Holiday Monday:

> 'All the wives and relatives of the men turned up at the camp to visit their menfolk. The camp was empty and they walked up to the Fort in the hope of seeing (them) and no doubt having a pleasant day. The Fort gates were shut and all ranks confined to barracks, so they gathered in little groups on the Fort banks, their wives etc. gathered on the footpath which ran along the other side of the moat and the conversation went along these lines shouted over the distance,
>
> "Can't you come out?"
>
> "NO"
>
> "You can"
>
> "I can't"
>
> "When will you come home?"
>
> "We don't know"
>
> This went on for some time much to the amusement of us younger men who were unattached. Tragically some of them never did return to Home and those that did although perhaps not wounded, remained scarred in mind and body but such is war'.
>
> 'The 1914-18 war was on us and the Fort at Newhaven was to be our home to us, on and off, for the next five years. On because it was our Depot to which we returned after postings to various duties, and off when we were away with duties which were to take us to B.E.F. France, Mesopotamia and many other theatres. Anyway the first thing after we had crossed the bridge and marched under the long archway into the square was to man the guns and battery posts.

Here we stood for about a week sleeping and living as best we could so as to be at instant readiness. In the meantime the rest of the organisation was to be carried out, barrack rooms prepared, gun crews detailed and generally getting down to prepare for what turned out to be a long stay, although everyone said it would all be over by Christmas.

Life then began to settle down. The barracks were allotted and men where able to live. We had good bedding with iron folding bedsteads, three palliasses, which made the bed and were known as biscuits, two army issue blankets, two linen sheets, one pillow and pillowslip. These and the bedstead had to be folded up every day and with the kit and rifle in their racks they were inspected every morning together with the cleanliness of the room which was swept out every day and wet scrubbed once a week with "Strongers" and hard scrubbers.

Physical training was carried out each morning before breakfast on the hard under the Fort under the instruction of my father [Charles George Cornford B.S.M] and between the two guns was a dummy loader where gun crews competed with each other as to the number of shells, each weighing one hundred and two pounds, could be loaded in one minute'

Corporal C.E. Cornford R.G.A

THE FORT LAYOUT AND ACCOMMODATION

By 1914 the men's dining hall and cookhouse were in a hut within the parade ground with a canteen in another hut beside the dormitory. There was no mains electricity at the Fort (this was not installed until 1939!).

'The Fort was illuminated in all barrack rooms, dining rooms, sergeants mess, guard room, canteens etc. by a Petrol Gas generating plant in the small compartment on the right hand side of the archway just inside the Fort gates. This consisted of two hot air engines run by the old barrack warden Bob Crick who lived in a cottage under the cliffs. He was quite a character, an old retired pensioned soldier who had served his time in the army and had many a rare tale to tell, especially to us youngsters. The throbbing of these little engines continued throughout the hours of darkness.'

Corporal C.E. Cornford R.G.A

'Our accommodation was reasonably tidy and clean but the coastguards, who also lived at the fort, had cleaner living quarters. We gunners worked 24 hour

> shifts and we slept in hammocks slung above the guns when on shift. There was always someone on lookout duty.'
>
> Gunner John Williamson R.G.A.

The gas was from the Town main, supplied by the Newhaven Gas & Coke Company whose offices were in Railway Road. The gas meter was situated at the corner of the Newhaven Recreation Ground, at the foot of the road leading to the Fort entrance. The main Gas stop cock was situated in the Engine House at the bottom of the archway entrance to the Fort.

> 'Leading off the square were the barrack rooms, one to sixteen, ablution rooms, Sergeant's Mess, Guard Room, complete with cells for Offenders, Officers Mess and Lounge, Wet and Dry Canteens, Cookhouse, Dining Room, Battery Office, Sergeant Major's Quarters, Master Gunner's Quarters and Artificer's Workshop. The Master Gunner's Office was situated on the West Bank. Leading off the battery parade were the steps leading to the guns floors and shelters, the steps to the B.C. post with the Le Clanche battery room under, gun stores ammunition rooms and room where men off duty slept in hammocks.
>
> Next to the B.C. post was the Coast Guard Station with its flag pole installation on the West bank above. The Coast Guards were at that time dressed in seaman uniforms with their Lieutenant and Petty Officers in the rig of the day. Their quarters next to the Sheffield Hotel in the Fort Road were married quarters and consisted of a row of meticulously clean cottages with a large flagstaff in the front and each cottage with its own beautifully kept cottage garden. They changed watch like us every twenty four hours.'
>
> Corporal C.E. Cornford R.G.A

The original design of the Fort did not include recreation rooms for the men – not even a bar. The soldiers, therefore, mixed with the towns people and this continued even though the soldiers' living quarters had been improved; four baths had been added and a 'recreation room' established. Rations to the Fort were supplied by lorry from Brighton.

> 'During my spell of duty at the Fort there was organised a small string band and concert party which gave entertainment to the public in the gymnasium,

attendance of the local church parades and joining in the local sports.'

Corporal C.E. Cornford R.G.A

Charles George Cornford, Battery Sergeant Major was an important N.C.O.:

'My father was, of course, responsible for the complete running, general cleanliness, discipline, training and tidiness of barrack rooms, Fort and general efficiency of the whole unit. He was also responsible to administer, fairly, leave to troops when possible, listen to their tales of woe and many other duties. It was not easy and, of course, I was given no kind of preference.

He was made a Second Class Warrant Officer and it was always difficult for me not to call him Dad as I had been used but as he told me very severely one day when I had been a little careless,

"You stand to attention Boy and say Sir when you address me."

The other men who were about at the time regarded this as fair and until I had to start out on my postings as a gunner and afterwards as an N.C.O. more or less adopted me under their care. I benefitted a lot from their characters. Life for a boy of fifteen years had hit Life with a bump.'

Corporal C.E. Cornford R.G.A.

The Fort boasted four six inch naval guns and a sergeant major, a great enthusiast, who spent hours each day showing us how to handle the weapons. I never once heard him swear, although our military stupidity must have tried his patience hard at times.

'Fetch a piece of four by two,' he shouted at me once, pointing to a heap of assorted timber. I had no idea what he meant and said so. He patiently explained and showed me a piece. I felt very ignorant and I take off my hat to his self control.

Gunner J Williamson R.G.A

In 1917 Battery Sergeant Major C.G. Cornford was presented with a silver mounted Sussex Artillery presentation parade cane. It was described as having "a silver knopped head, the top engraved with initials 'CGC', the sides with scrolling foliage, and a middle band engraved 'Presented to S M Cornford by NCO's and men of No 2 Coy Sussex RGA, Newhaven, 1917'."

CALLED TO THE BATTERY OFFICE

'On my second day at the Fort a sergeant came into the barrack room with a message. 'Gunner Williamson, you're wanted at the battery office at once, and I mean at once' he shouted, and out he went. In my innocence I thought he meant at once.

I had no puttees on and was wearing brown canvas shoes, Army issue, and no cap. It was cold, so I flung my tunic over my shoulders and ran across the parade ground to the office. I knocked and a voice said 'Come in'. I entered and said 'Someone wants to see me, I'm told'.

To my astonishment a sergeant sitting at a desk jumped to his feet and looked as though he would burst with rage. He let out a roar: 'What the ----. Stand to attention. How dare you come into this office half naked! Go and get dressed properly and return here.'

I returned to the barrack room reflecting that in this strange military world 'at once' didn't mean at once'.

Gunner J Williamson R.G.A

THE MASTER GUNNER

'The armaments and general equipment of the Fort came under the care and very strict supervision of the Master Gunner, Master Gunner Larking who had been a regular Master Gunner in the Royal Garrison Artillery. He wore the regular Long Service Medal and was on a service pension. He was the proprietor of a tobacconist shop called Uncle Tom's Cabin in Ship Street, Brighton and had joined the Territorials.'

Corporal. C.E. Cornford R.G.A.

'The master gunner, a man we rarely saw, was highly praised by the new C.O. when his magazine below ground was inspected. It was there that he spent most of his time, a human mole. There were numerous shells in wooden racks, each one dusted and, I'll swear, even polished by this enthusiast in whose care they were. He was, I imagine, quite upset when a large consignment had to be loaded on lorries and sent off, presumably to France, where there was a shortage of these missiles.'

Gunner J Williamson R.G.A

'Shortly after mobilisation orders were received that we were to reduce to battery strength of 120 ranks, 2 Trumpeters and one boy. All unfit men, Bandsmen surplus to requirements, trumpeters over strength etc were to be sent home. I was the one Boy retained to continue with the battery.

Next to occur was that we were asked to volunteer for overseas service and having signed for this occasion which would carry with it a bounty of twenty five pounds when Peace was restored and we were demobilised. We signed and were paid the King's Bounty of £5 in Golden Sovereigns.... We were then issued with a Silver Bar with imperial service embossed upon it and a crown mounted on the bar which we wore on the left breast.

The Trumpeters of No. 1 Depot had not been drafted and each morning we had to join them under Trumpet Major Tommy Lyons and Corporal Greenhall in the valley beyond the married quarters for trumpet practice unless we were detailed for Trumpeter of the Guard, when for twenty four hours we slept in the Guard Room under the orders of the Corporal of the guard and sounded off all calls for the battery, Parades, Cookhouse, Postman's Call, Officer's Dinner, Sunset, First and Last Post and Lights Out etc. etc. , or you were detailed for Battery Trumpeter when you were detailed to the Battery Commander's Post and for whom you acted as a Runner'.

Corporal C.E. Cornford

On mobilisation the Standing Orders for the Officer on duty and look-out men in the Fort were as follows:

Officer on duty He will come on duty at 8 a.m. daily and receive a report from the officer coming off duty.
He will inspect the look-out men and guard before marching off.
He will visit the guard once by day and at least twice by night.
He will frequently visit the look-out men by day and night.
He will carry out the orders for the Examination Battery.

Look-out Men Two will be posted in the best position for observation, near the B.C. Post.
They will at once report to the officer on duty the approach of any vessel.

Their tour of duty will be for two hours, but at the end of the first hour, the next man will come on duty, and for the second hour there will be two look-out men, e.g.
1st look-out man. 8 a.m. – 10 a.m.
2nd look-out man 9 a.m. – 11 a.m.
3rd look-out man 10 a.m. – 12 noon.
In thick or very cold weather it may be found necessary to reduce the tour of duty to one hour.

THE EXAMINATION SERVICE

'There was one other service which I should mention which we carried out, this was the Examination Service. This consisted of Signallers in parties which we sent to the Examination Boat under the command of Captain Pascoe who commanded the L.B.S.C.R Tug "Alert". Their job being to examine incoming shipping to Newhaven Harbour and giving them permission to enter, if in order, whilst flying three coloured lights of red and white lights by night on a changing twenty four hour basis or when it was thought security was broken, each boat using a different sequence of flags and lights.

I myself could use the Morse and Semifore (sic) codes and obtained permission to spend some of my days off guard on gun floor duty with the "Alert". While not cruising up and down off Newhaven we drifted and fished and we had a lot of good catches which supplemented our rations and some went to the Officer's Mess Cook Reggie Payne for a few pence to supplement our pocket money".

WATCH DUTIES

'My duties also included watches spent in the B.C. (Battery Command) post as a range finder and with responsibility to watch for the recognition signal of the boats entering the port. This was a critical duty as the port of Newhaven was a major ammunition and supply port for the army of the B.E.F. in France and if an enemy vessel entered and blew itself up, the effect on our war in France would have been devastating.

I well remember one night when it was my duty to carry out this observation, I saw a vessel approaching the port and the signal which was at night Red, White, White and I observed it was correct. When it reached the lighthouse tide signal station below the Fort I noticed that it appeared Red and White only. My heart missed many beats as to what the consequence might be and it would have been at my faulting. Somewhat in a panic I ran to Fort Hill, the sentry on duty thinking I had gone somewhat mad, as if I could prevent a catastrophe at this stage, when to my utter relief and near collapse I could then see that the lower white had smoked up, as most of the ships only had oil lamps in those days. I was to prove only a small matter to what I was to experience in France when my life took me to the front line. But it taught me one very serious thing, BE THOROUGH IN ALL THINGS no matter how minor, and when in my latter life as an engineer I always checked what my hand would do before I let it move especially in matters electrical.'

Corporal C.E. Cornford

'Some yards from the guns was the BC (Battery Command) post, a small room fitted with a range finder and an electrical gadget for passing the range to the gun layers, as well as telescopes and binoculars. Joined to it was the coastguard's room, manned by a Chief Petty Officer and a rating. The two rooms were sunk into the cliff top with only windows showing above ground.

Each ship that passed was examined by armed trawler crews and if the vessel was to enter Newhaven Harbour, it was given certain flags to fly. . Each day we were given a new code word, for instance, IMAGINATION. The first ship flew IMA the next GIN and so on. At night red and white lights were hoisted to the mastheads instead of flags.

One terrible foggy night, a large steamer was flying the correct lights but I thought it was coming in on the wrong side of the harbour wall. I ran next door and expressed my concern. The Chief Petty Officer used his binoculars, stronger than mine and confirmed my suspicions. He immediately sent by signal lamp UUUU which meant "You are running into danger". After several seconds, the ship answered and reversed its engines, just in time to save it from grounding on the beach.

On another memorable occasion we spotted out at sea, the periscope of a submarine. Immediately the alarm was given, warning flags were hoisted and the guns loaded. We followed the periscope on the range finder, as did the guns. But we were not allowed to fire without permission from the garrison commander. No one knew where he was, so we saw our target slipping away.

> The Navy had no such inhibitions and two destroyers went tearing out of the harbour at full speed, causing waves which sank several small boats. By this time, the periscope had disappeared but the destroyers dropped a number of depth charges sending huge spouts of water up into the air. We were never told of the outcome of it all. The gun crews then had the dangerous job of unloading the guns.
>
> Gunner J Williamson R.G.A

On one occasion a ship failed to stop or answer signals and the order was given to open fire on it with one of the 6in. guns; the ship was hit and a crew member slightly injured, but at least the ship stopped!

RANGE FINDING

The battery at Newhaven was 187 feet above mean sea level and with quite a large rise and fall of tide this had to be counteracted. This was carried out as follows. A datum post painted in black and white was situated under Seaford Head, the man on watch at the Depression Range Finder made a sighting through his telescope with its crossed wires of spider's web cutting the foot line where the level of the sea met it, his range bar then being set to the range of the datum post. He then adjusted his state of tide drum at the rear of the instrument to the water line and read them off the level of the tide. The guns were 6 inch B.L. Mark VII and were fitted with a tide lever inside the shield and the conversation, shouted against a strong wind in many cases, went like this:

"A.I. tide fall of three", reply

"A.I. tide fall of three, Sir, last motion one of up"

Whereupon the gunner on watch would release the clamp of the tide lever and move the lever to the mark on the brass scale to fall of three and making sure that his last motion of the lever was one motion of UP. This was to ensure that the slack on the cam of the sight which the tide lever operated was taken up, (this was) a very essential precaution. At night time the Engineers at the end of the breakwater would expose the searchlight to illuminate the datum for us.

GUARD DUTIES

C.E. Cornford was promoted to Corporal:

'Duties were divided between the battery as a gun layer and corporal of the Guard in the guard room at the gate entrance. This entailed the relieving of sentries posted on the land side of the moat, ensuring that they understood their orders and listening for any sign of them being disturbed during their two hour watch and at the end of their watch seeing that they changed at the precise time. Any deviation from these principles would provoke some adverse comment. There were also many visits from a young lady (who) had just left school, employed by the Post Office as a Telegraph Girl and it was one of her duties to bring the Fort official telegrams etc. It was an arduous task for such a young lady but she took it in her stride and delivered them in all types of adverse weather conditions on her heavy Post Office bike with her heavy great coat. Her name at that time was Miss Grace Christmas and I took the telegrams from her when it was my turn on guard duty.'

Corporal C.E. Cornford

On my first sentry duty, I was posted at the end of the wooden bridge leading to the fort entrance across the empty moat. It was specially emphasised that no one, not even an officer, was to be allowed into the Fort without a pass.
At about 10 o'clock a strange officer approached, I saluted and politely asked him for his pass.

'Whatever next?' he said angrily, 'I'm the garrison commander'.

He was wearing an officer's uniform but I could see no insignia of rank anywhere.

'I'm sorry sir,' I said 'but my instructions are that no one enters the fort without a pass'.

He attempted to walk on across the bridge so I blocked his path with rifle at the ready and shouted 'Guard! Turn out! to the rest of the guard in the guard room next to the gateway. They did so and presented arms. I shouted to the bombardier in charge that this officer wouldn't produce a pass. He came running towards me.

'He's the garrison commander, you fool,' he shouted. 'Let him in.' What the bombardier called me afterwards cannot be printed, but I still maintain that I acted properly. I expected a wigging from high authority but none came.

The stupid thing about this sentry post was that at night the sentry was fully illuminated by an electric light above him, which meant that oncomers (sic) could see him yards away, while he could not see who was approaching, so that he had to challenge into the darkness guided by the sound of footsteps or voices.

The whole arrangement was useless really because at the opposite side of the Fort there was a small door unlocked, through which a soldier late home from the town could enter without being seen or heard. I wonder if the Germans knew! We all did.'

Gunner J Williamson R.G.A

FORMATION OF 2 COMPANY SUSSEX R.G.A.

As the war progressed and the need for men greatly increased occupants from the R.G.A. in the Fort were posted to serve in Royal Garrison Artillery units overseas. The Fort, therefore, undertook the training of men for overseas duty. A 2nd Sussex R.G.A. Company was formed in 1917. The Strength Return of 17th April 1917 shows that No. 1 Company consisted of 2 Officers and 95 men and No. 2 Company 4 officers and 96 men.

'The war took on a different meaning and we had to form a second company in Brighton so that the first company at the Fort could be sent to form Siege Batteries for the B.E.F in France. Sergeant Major Jimmy Wallis was sent from the Fort to carry out this task at Gloucester Road.

Soon after, the second company were posted to Newhaven among them my father's brother, Uncle Bill who was a sergeant.'

[William Henry Cornford, Acting Sergeant 374215 No.2 Company, Sussex R.G.A. was posted to Newhaven on 26th May 1917]

'Out of No. 1 Company we had then formed personnel for two Siege Batteries for the B.E.F. in France, 69th Siege Battery of 9.2 inch Howitzers and 122nd Siege Battery of 6 inch Howitzers. No. 2 Company had relieved us and many of my Brighton friends had gone, men from the Brighton Tramways, Post Office, L.B. & S.C.R. Railway and many other organisations from Brighton and its environments.

....many (men) of No. 2 Company were posted to various theatres of war and new faces of less fit men were under the care of my father and the Master Gunner and Officers had changed.'

Corporal C.E. Cornford

THE VISIT OF THE INSPECTING GENERAL

'One day we had a warning that the inspecting general of the district was to pay us a visit to see that we were all clean and tidy, quite an unnecessary item in our case with the Warrant Officers and Master Gunner as we had. Anyway, he duly arrived with his trailing retinue, when at the gate of the Fort his eyes lit up with dismay as the only flag in evidence was the White Ensign on its mast and yardarm of the Royal Navy Coastguards. He resolutely refused to cross the drawbridge whilst that flag was the only flag in evidence. What was to be done? The Master Gunner rose to the occasion, being a man of some resourcefulness. A long pole was obtained and white-washed, this was mounted over the gate in a hole in the ground and to its top was hauled a Union Jack. This being accomplished his greatness deigned to cross the drawbridge and enter the Fort to see how we small fry were behaving.'

Corporal C.E. Cornford

CAMOUFLAGING THE FORT

'Our C.O., a major, decided that the Fort should be camouflaged and we spent a long time painting the exterior walls of the barrack room with patches of yellow, brown and green paint so that they would not be easily seen from any German aircraft. We also had to use alternate paths to the guns so that the well-worn short cuts would quickly be clothed in weeds and grass. The whole fort soon took on a non-lived-in appearance.

One day the C.O. was transferred to another battery and a new major arrived – a pukka sahib this one – an old regular soldier who sported a monocle. Rumour had it that on his arrival he exclaimed: 'Good God, what a slovenly looking place! Camouflage? Rubbish! Don't you think the Germans know it's here? Then why hide it?

Immediately the grass and weeds had to be removed from the paths which were then edged with large stones and whitewashed.'.

Gunner J Williamson R.G.A

OFFICERS OF THE SUSSEX R.G.A.

The following Sussex R.G.A. officer's attended the Dinner of the Sussex R.G.A. in the Mess at Newhaven Fort on Christmas Day 1914:

A.J.M. Martineau	Major, Commanding Officer at the time
W.H. Grinsted	Captain (On 'Newhaven Fortress News' committee, became the C.O. of 1/1 Company)
W.A. Dow	Lieutenant (became the C.O. of 2/1 Company)
K.G. Roberts	Lieutenant
Beaumont	Lieutenant
G.J.Jones	Second Lieutenant
J.E. Montgomery	Second Lieutenant
R.W.V. Thunder	Second Lieutenant
R. Hill Shaw	Captain (Medical Officer)

Manning a Newhaven Fort 6 inch gun [NFA]

N.C.O. s of the Sussex R.G.A. at the Fort September 1914 . Battery Sergeant Major Charles George Cornford is believed to be on the front row third from left, without the moustache.[NFA]

The Tug 'ALERT' towing out Newhaven built brigantine 'SUSSEX MAID' circa 1912 [NMM]

The lighthouse at the end of the breakwater, Newhaven Harbour [NFA]

Searchlight emplacement West Beach – demolished in the 1960s [NFA]

Group of Sussex R.G.A. men in parade ground of camouflaged Fort [NFA]

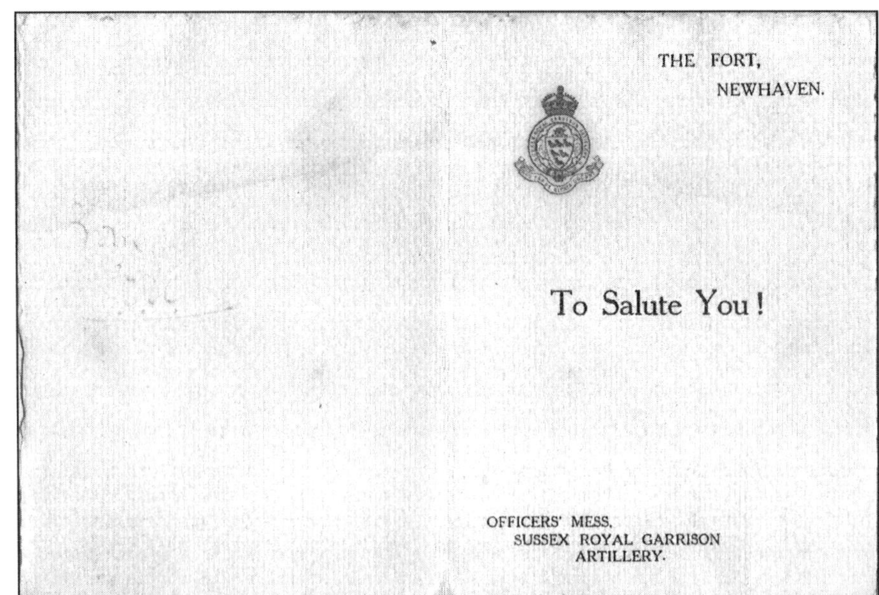
THE FORT,
NEWHAVEN.

To Salute You!

OFFICERS' MESS,
SUSSEX ROYAL GARRISON
ARTILLERY.

Christmas card sent by the officers of the Sussex R.G.A. [NFA]

FORT COMMANDING OFFICERS 1914-1918

The following officers have been identified as having served as the commanding officer of the companies of the Sussex R.G.A. in Newhaven.

1. Major Alfred John Martineau - Commander 1/1 Company Sussex R.G.A. 26th Aug 1914 to 15th November 1915

Alfred John Martineau was born in 1871, the youngest son of Judge Alfred and Maria Martineau, 6 Evelyn Terrace, Brighton. He was educated at St. Thomas's Hospital, taking the M.R.C.S. and L.R.C.P. London in 1895, and also the F.R.C.S. Edinburgh in 1899. After filling the posts of house-surgeon at St. Thomas's Hospital, and at the Hospital for Sick Children, Great Ormond Street, and of house-physician to the Brompton Chest Hospital, he went into practice at Hove, Sussex, where he was surgeon to the Brighton Ear and Throat Hospital. Alfred Martineau had served for many years in No.1 (Brighton) Company of the Sussex Territorial Royal Garrison Artillery. On August 26th 1914 he was promoted to the rank of major and to the command of the company. During the early part of the war he was stationed at Newhaven, in command of the fort.

Major Martineau had relinquished command by 15th November 1915 when (it is believed that) Major W F H Grinsted took over command. Major Martineau was posted to another unit, possibly the 19th Siege Battery, Royal Garrison Artillery which had gone to France in May 1915. He went to France on 7th April 1916, as shown by his medal index card.

He was killed in action on April 17th 1917 aged 46 whilst with the 19th Siege Battery, Royal Garrison Artillery. He was shot by a sniper whilst doing reconnaissance work in connection with his battery. He is buried at the Bully-Grenay Communal Cemetery, British Extension, Bully-les-Mines, Pas de Calais.

His home address was 22, Cambridge Road, Hove at the time of his death.

'I learnt the news that one of our best liked Officers of prewar days, a Major Martineau, who in happier days had been a leading surgeon at the Children's

Throat and Ear hospital in Upper Church Street, Brighton, had been killed in France while marking the fall of shot of a German battery. A Great Loss'

Corporal C. E. Cornford, Sussex R.G.A.

2. Major William Frank Harrison Grinsted – Commander 1/1 Company, Sussex R.G.A. from 15th Nov 1915 to April 1916.

William Grinsted was a Territorial Officer in the Sussex R.G.A. before the outbreak of the war and volunteered for overseas service in August 1914. He was promoted to Temporary Captain on 2nd November 1914 and appointed to command No.2 Armoured Train Company in April 1915. He was then promoted to Temporary Major and assumed command of 1/1 Company Sussex R.G.A. on 15th Nov 1915. He reverted to Captain in April 1916 transferring to 122 Siege Battery R.G.A. as second-in-command to go overseas. He arrived with the Battery in France on 18th July 1916.

Major Grinsted saw service in France throughout the war and was awarded the M.C. finishing up as Acting Lieutenant Colonel In command of 66th Brigade R.G.A. He was demobilized on 27th February 1919.

3. Major William Alexander Dow, Sussex R.G.A. – Commander 2/1st Company, Sussex R.G.A. 24th July 1915 to 14th Feb 1917

Dr W.A. Dow was born in Kidderminster, Worcs. , on 25th Feb 1868. By 1912 he was living in Lewes and was a medical practitioner in partnership with Doctors Benton and Crosskey.

On 9th July 1912 Dr. Dow applied for a commission with the Sussex R.G.A (T.F.) (he had also been nominated for the R.A.M.C.). On 10th July 1912 he was appointed as a Second Lieutenant in the Sussex R.G.A. (London Gazette 6th Aug 1912 Page 5858)

On mobilization in August 1914, Second Lieutenant Dow took up his military duties and Dr Benton carried on the practice.

By 24th July 1915 he was now Lieutenant (Temporary Major) commanding Newhaven Fort with the Sussex R.G.A. He was responsible for defence work and continuous training of recruits and for sending them to new formations.

On 16th October 1916 Major Dow wrote to the Newhaven Garrison

Commander Lieutenant Colonel Hankey enquiring into the possibility of his resigning his commission or transferring to the reserve on compassionate grounds. He was in financial difficulties, facing bankruptcy if he could not return to his practice. Dr. Crosskey had retired with an agreed annuity of £250 per annum and Dr. Benton had died suddenly. Major Dow was legally obliged to pay Dr Benton's estate £250 p.a. for two years. Local doctors had looked after the practice's patients temporarily but this could not continue as they were overworked. Finding a locum was impossible as was the selling of the practice.

Lieutenant Colonel Hankey, Garrison Commander, forwarded Major Dow's letter to the Major General I.C. Administration, Eastern Command with the annotation 'Forwarded for favour of consideration. This seems to be a very genuine case'.

On 30th November 1916 Eastern Command informed the War Office that owing to the shortage of medical men it recommended that a special case can be made out to allow Maj. Dow to resign his combatant commission if he placed his professional services as a medical man at the disposal of the state for part-time service. It was proposed that he be employed as a part-time Civil Medical Practitioner at the York Place Hospital in Brighton at £250 p.a.

On 5th January 1917 the Central Medical War Committee, War Office reported that they had made enquiries about Maj. Dow's practice and confirmed that it was not possible for other practices in the neighbourhood to take on his patients and recommended his demobilisation and his part-time employment as a Civil Medical Practitioner.

On 14th February 1917 Maj. Dow was demobilised and transferred to the T.F. Reserve. He retained his rank of Major. He retired from the T.F. Reserve having reached the age limit on 27th September 1921.

50 ANTI-AIRCRAFT COMPANY R.G.A. NEWHAVEN FORT

The company is listed in the Daily Strength Return of Newhaven Garrison of 13th April 1917 as having 5 officers and 50 men present with establishment strength of 9 officers and 139 men. However, the company is not included in the Newhaven Defence Scheme (Revised to 1918).

A Nordenfelt 6 pounder anti-aircraft gun was mounted in the Fort for a period during the war so it is probable that this company manned this gun. However, it is unlikely that so many men were required to maintain and operate a single gun of this type.

An AA Section serving overseas consisted of 43 men in total: 2 officers, two gun detachments of 12 men each (of which 1 in each was a Driver of the ASC), 2 telephonists, 1 linesman, 4 height finders, 4 Wilson-Dalby Detector Operators, 2 Height and Fuze Indicator men, 1 Order Board Setter, 1 Lookout man (Air sentry), 1 orderly and 1 cook. All RGA unless indicated.

It is probable, therefore, that the company was primarily in Newhaven for training purposes rather than the actual defence of the Fort.

The plan "The Armament of the Fort during W.W.1" from Newhaven Museum (see Appendix) shows the location of a 6 pounder anti-aircraft gun with the notation "(1915-16)". It is possible, therefore, that the Nordenfelt gun was still in the Fort in early 1917 being removed some time between April and November of that year since a large diagram of the Fort layout produced by Sapper H.H. Philcox, R.E. on 1st November 1917 does not show the presence of the AA gun. (National Archives Ref. MPH 1/981, copy in Fort Archives)

The Nordenfelt 6 pounder anti-aircraft gun was becoming obsolete and was withdrawn from service in 1919.

With guns that had not been designed for the purpose and appropriate equipment late in being developed, the AA was perhaps more of a deterrent than an actually effective weapon. The complexities of deflection firing, weather conditions, target fixing, variable gun condition, etc made for a very difficult operation. Training was all too brief, and methods experimental. Most of the gun Sections arrived in the field of battle without having fired a live shot. One source says that for example, in the busy week ending 27 April 1918, a total of 10 enemy aircraft were shot down and another 5 damaged, of a total of 2039 engaged.

No specific information about 50 Anti-Aircraft company's activities or personnel has been found.

FORTRESS COMPANY, ROYAL ENGINEERS

TERRITORIAL FORCE – FORT HILL CAMP

On 1August 1914 there were 11 Fortress Companies in the UK and 15 overseas, all on coastal defence duties. Some were entirely for Electric Light (that is, searchlight) duty; others also had Works responsibilities. On mobilisation, men of the Territorial RE took over the home stations, releasing men for duty with the British Expeditionary Force - although not all regulars were withdrawn right away but were released gradually, their places being filled by men who were unfit for overseas service. Territorial troops also moved out to take over some of the overseas stations.

Under the Haldane Army Reforms introduced in 1908 the Territorial Force unit for Newhaven was the Sussex Fortress Engineers. It would appear safe to assume, therefore, that Newhaven men would have served in this Fortress Company.

The work of the Royal Engineers in a Fortress during Peace Time was as follows:-

1. Erection, maintenance and running of defence electric lights, both fixed and mobile
2. Erection, maintenance and working of the military telephone system, except those portions which were maintained by the Post Office in Great Britain and Ireland.
3. Construction and maintenance of fortifications and permanent entrenchments, including living accommodation for their garrisons; military roads; magazines and storehouses; sites for camps.

The work during War Time was a continuation of the peace duties on a larger and more strenuous scale. Thus:

1. Electric lights will be run all night for many nights in succession.
2. Additional telephone lines must be run and offices opened to link up the extra defences to be constructed. Telephone exchanges must be manned night and day.
3. Forts must be prepared for war; musketry parapets completed; obstacles erected or improved; dressing stations arranged; reserve water supply and adequate sanitary services provided for the war garrisons.
4. As barracks will in many cases continue to be occupied, their maintenance, especially of the water and sanitary services, must be continued as in peace. Some of the barracks may have to be converted to hospitals.
5. The schemes for strengthening the defences must be put into effect; entrenchments constructed; as these may have to be occupied for some weeks, special attention must be paid to surface drainage, water storage and sanitation, and in many cases the shelters in works may develop into semi-permanent buildings of iron and concrete.

The training of the R.E. was composed of:
Engineer Training
i) Technical training for electric light and telephone duties.
ii) Training in "Works"
iii) Training in "Fieldworks"
And Military Training
iv) Drill and field training as an infantry company
v) Musketry, visual training and ranging
vi) Signalling
vii) Engineer reconnaissance and map reading.

A New Years dinner of the 2/1st Sussex (Fortress) Royal Engineers was held on 7th Jan 1916 and was reported in detail in the local press. See the Appendix for a copy of the newspaper report and a list of all men who attended.

The Garrison Daily Strength return dated 13th April 1917 show that there were 4 officers and 178 O.R.s in 2/1 Company Sussex (Fortress) R.E.

Fortress Company R.E. - Sapper E.W. Tyler holding spade 3rd from left [NMM]

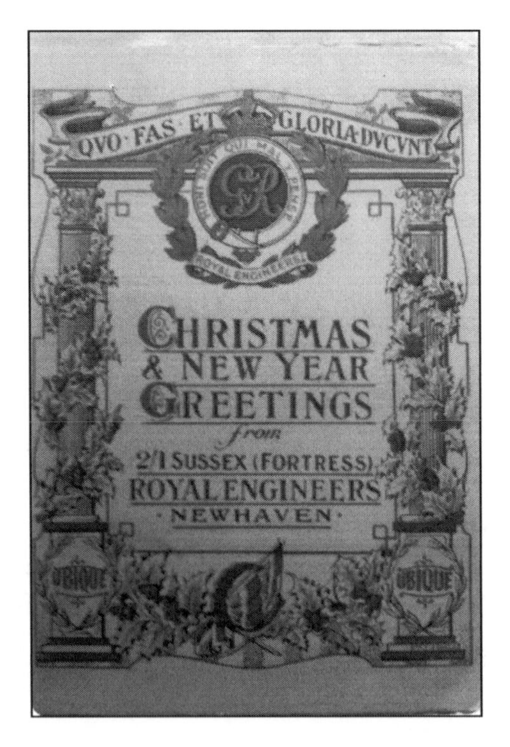

Christmas card from 2/1 Sussex (Fortress) Royal Engineers from Newhaven [NMM]

4 COMPANY LONDON ELECTRICAL ENGINEERS
R.E. T.F. IN NEWHAVEN FORT

The London Electrical Engineers, Royal Engineers, Territorial Force consisted of an HQ and 6 Companies and was based in 46, Regency Street, Westminster.

Major A.E. Levin was the C.O. in Newhaven in November 1915 and Captain T.H. Vitty was one of his officers.

The responsibility of this unit of the Fortress Company R.E. was to man the searchlights under the tactical control of the Battery Commander. The lights consisted of two 90 cm Projectors - Clarke Chapman Lamps.

A member of this Company recalled his time at Newhaven between 1914 and 1916 in a document entitled 'Notes on the Newhaven Coastal Fort during 1914-1916'.

> June 25th 1914. Fort occupied by small section of Territoral London Electrical Engineers in addition to a Sussex Royal Garrison Artillery Coy. resident in the Fort.
>
> August 4th war declared & all but half a dozen T.R.E. Londoners sent back to London H.Q. for dispersal to other coastal areas in Britain. At midnight the General Alarm was sounded & 3 T.R.E.s including self despatched to end of Breakwater to run searchlights, first to start up 40 B.H.P Crossley Engines in Engine House & one electrician in each of the 16 ton turrets to run the 90 cm searchlights.
>
> All passed peaceably & indeed for subsequent nights. Searchlights continued to be run i.e. shown out searching 120 degrees left & right for the remainder of 1914 & part of 1915 without particular incident, save one night late in 1915 in a heavy storm, when my turret was traversed broadside on to an exceptionally heavy wave, which shattered the half inch thick plate glass through which the beam was shining, smashing the searchlight mirror & nearly drowning a sapper & myself. We had the presence of mind to roll back the heavy steel shutter before the next wave caught us.

There was a courts martial, the result of which was never made public as far as I remember. I would add that, at times in a very rough weather, the effect of countless heavy seas thudding down on the roof of the turret was frightening & almost as un-nerving as the blast of the fog horn a yard outside the turret during a six hour shift.

One further incident I recall, when a small yacht in daytime refused to answer signals from the battery command post in the Fort. The R.G.A. Lt. ordered the guns to be fired, scoring a hit on the yacht & causing a casualty therein. Jolly good gunners the R.G.A!

Life for us engineers was pleasant enough in the early part of the war although conditions were not so pleasant when yanked out of bed at 2 a.m. (third shift) to don oilskins & wade through sea water which would be sucked under the breakwater arches totally immersing us (one chap lost his eyeglasses) roped together in rough weather.

In spare time when confined to barracks a few of us clubbed together & rented a piano from Brighton, one of us being a first class pianist, another a violinist & many happy hours were spent around the piano with songs brought from home.

After due warning to coastal shipping, periodic target practice with the two six inch guns was carried out by the R.G.A. gunners at appropriate ranges, town residents being warned to open windows.

Heavily armoured cables fitted under the breakwater arches, supplied current for telephones & the servo-electric control of the hydraulic rams operating the turrets, maximum traverse being 120 degrees left and right. Electric power for the two searchlight lamp carbons (120 amps x 60 volts) was provided by generators directly coupled to the 40 H.P. Crossley engines in the engine room. Servicing & cleaning the searchlights and engines was a mornings job & we were then generally free of duty until the night shift.

Our small complement of T.R.E. officers & men were reinforced from London H.Q. from time to time to replace those of us sent to France & elsewhere. We had little contact with the gunners being housed in separate barrack rooms.

The dry moat provided a 100 yards shooting range, competitions in which I was luckily successful, being held from time to time. Leaving Newhaven in 1916 I regret I can furnish no further information as to what transpired later.

An R.G.A man also recalled his memories of the Electrical Engineers.

'We had by this time been joined by the section of London Territorials, The London Electrical Engineers who were to run the searchlight emplacements at the base of the lighthouse at the end of the Breakwater. These were very large and powerful lights. I think in view of my later service with the R.N.V.R and experience of a searchlight burner they were 36 inch. These were run by two petrol driven generators in two engine rooms and quite early in the war a system was devised so that they could be controlled from the B.C. (Battery Command) Post in the Fort. This was done by means of which I have come to know as some form of William Janney variable oil pump gear, the control of the valves for traversing and elevation being carried out in the B.C. post to rotate the turrets containing the searchlights and control elevation. It could be a very tough job requiring some considerable nerve to run this installation especially with sweeping the sea many feet over the end of the Breakwater in the considerable gales which were very often experienced.

Then there was the very strong East gales which blew the exhaust fumes back through the ventilating fans into the engine rooms. The engine room on these occasions had to be evacuated. Then there were very often times when the relief watch had to lash themselves together with rope to make their way out under the archway to their posts to prevent them being washed over into the harbour bight and when they eventually did arrive they would find that a foot of sea water had to be stood in the engine room.

One of the sergeants was the son of Chater Lea and another the son of Lee Francis whose people were connected with the motor cycle industry. Their firms sent them a powerful motor cycle each on which they carried out despatch riding for the Garrison Commander when they were not required at their searchlight post.'

Corporal C.E. Cornford R.G.A

The Garrison strength return of 13th April 1917 gives the strength of No.4. Company London Electrical Engineers as 3 officers and 39 O.R.s.

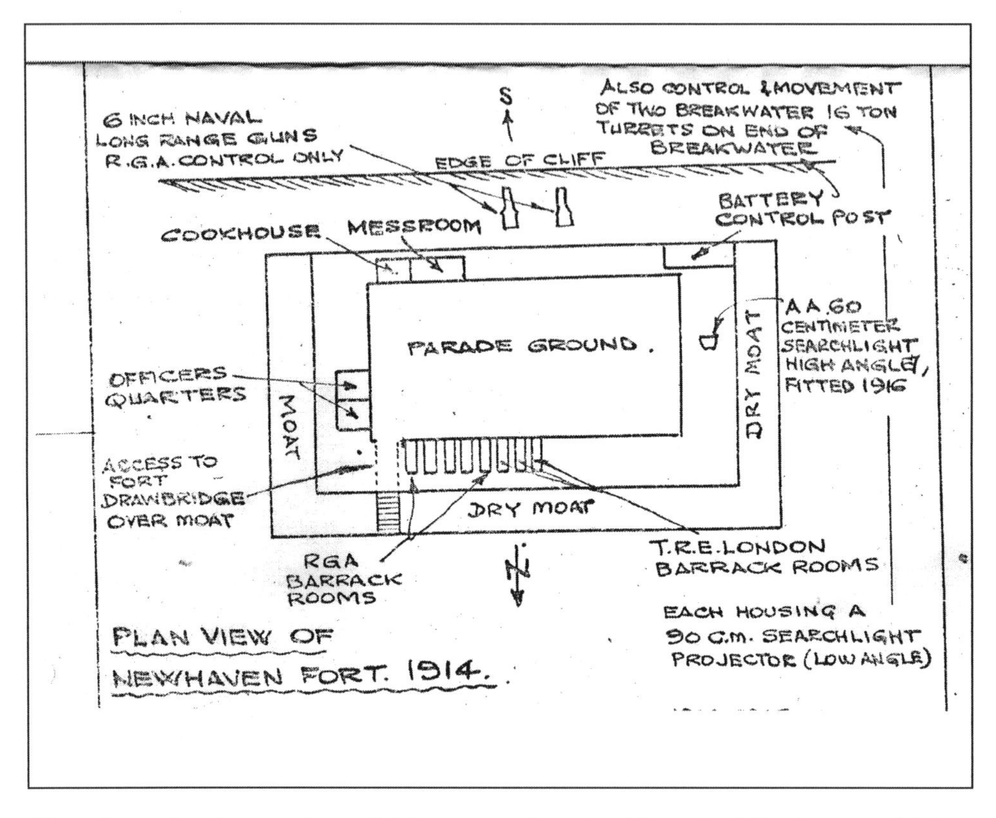

Plan drawn by the member of 4 Company, London Electrical Engineers which accompanied his memoirs [NFA]

The badge of the London Electrical Engineers drawn by Sapper L.H. Hall
ARS MARTIS COMES - "Art is the Companion of war" [NFA]

London Electrical Engineers R.E. postcard sent by Bombardier W H Balcombe, Sussex R.G.A. from Newhaven Fort in February 1916 [NFA]

SIGNALS R.E. T.F. IN NEWHAVEN FORT

The Signals, Royal Engineers, Territorial Force was responsible for telephone communications and despatch riders.

The Garrison strength return of 13th April 1917 shows that there were 4 O.R. Motor Cyclists in the Company and the establishment was 4.

Newspaper report on "Accident to a Territorial" – Sapper A.V. Tucknott 28th August 1914:

> "On Saturday evening Sapper Albert Victor Tucknott, a telegraphist in the Newhaven Half Company of the Sussex Fortress Royal Engineers (Territorials), met with an accident which, to his disappointment, will prevent him from taking any further part for some time in military activities.
> It appears that about 7.45 he was standing on the pavement in the High Street outside Messrs. J. Bannister & Sons new shop when a motor coach from Seaford struck him and knocked him into the gutter, and the near back wheel passed over his left foot. The boot was removed and Tucknott was carried into the shop, attended by Dr. J. McGlasan, and afterwards taken to his home at 12, Bridge Street. His foot was much bruised and swollen, but marvellous to state, no bones are believed to have been broken. Tucknott was wearing a strong pair of boots with particularly stout soles or, so it is thought, his injury would have been far more serious".

578 WORKS COMPANY SUSSEX FORTRESS ENGINEERS, R.E. FORT HILL CAMP

This company was one of a number of fortress companies in the UK and their prime purpose was to co-operate with companies of the Royal Garrison Artillery in the provision of coastal defence. The Works Company was to be available in reserve to provide any R.E. Services that the situation may require.

The company was formed in Seaford on 3rd October 1914 and was transferred to Newhaven on 21st January 1915 and was based at Fort Hill Camp. It remained in Newhaven until August 1918. The Company Commanding Officer was Captain F.C. Sanders R.E.

On 24th August 1918 the Company was notified to prepare for overseas service in France at the establishment for a Works Company, R.E., with the exception of the two buglers. The establishment was made up of 1 Captain, 2 Subalterns, one Sergeant Major, 4 Sergeants, 5 Corporals, 5 Second Corporals, four Lance Corporals and 73 Sappers making a total of 95 men. They were required for duty in France of a temporary but urgent nature and no special medical examination was required, the personnel being of any category except B (iii).

On 28th August 1918 it was reported to the War Office that the personnel were up to establishment, that clothing was up to requirements but that owing to the delay in receiving instructions regarding equipment none had yet been received.

On 6th September 1918 the Company was reported as being complete as regards personnel, clothing and equipment.

The Company was inspected on 7th September 1918 by Brigadier General Anley, Newhaven Garrison Commander and orders were received for the Company to proceed to Southampton by 8.47 am train on Monday 9th September 1918.

The Company arrived at Southampton at 4 pm on 9th September and proceeded to a rest camp. They then embarked on the 'Maid of Orleans' at 4 pm on 10th September 1918. On arriving at Le Havre at 1 am on 11th September they went to a rest camp from which on 13th September they boarded a train to SANGEVILLE at 2 pm (which left at 7.45 pm!!)

The Company then commenced their service in France. The officers recorded as being with the regiment were Captain F.C. Saunders and Lieutenants H.G. Warren and A.W. Kenyon.

C.S.M. Wells leading 578 Works Company, Sussex Fortress Engineers through Bridge Street, Newhaven. [NMM]

578 Works Company, Sussex Fortress Engineers June 1917 [NFA]

THE NEWHAVEN GARRISON

The men who served within the Newhaven Garrison belonged to many diverse units and not all units were stationed in Newhaven for the entire war. Additionally, the strength of each unit constantly changed.

GARRISON COMMANDERS

The Garrison Commander was responsible for the command of the Garrison, the enforcement in conjunction with the Senior Naval Officer of the Examination Service, the duties of Competent Military Authority No. 5 (Newhaven) and No. 11 Sussex Areas and the control of the Newhaven Special Military Area of which he was appointed Commandant.

The Garrison Headquarters were located at 63, Meeching Road, Newhaven.

The Garrison Headquarters establishment consisted of the Commandant, a Staff Captain (who had a riding horse at his disposal), 5 clerks (including a civilian Superintending Clerk and a Lance-Corporal) and two Batmen.

The following men are known to have served as Garrison Commander during the war:

1. Lieutenant Colonel G.R.M Church, Royal Artillery 5th Aug 1914 to 16th May 1915

On mobilisation Major Church relinquished command of No.1 Depot, R.G.A. which had been in Newhaven Fort and was appointed Newhaven Garrison Commander. He was promoted to the temporary rank of Lieutenant Colonel on 20th August 1914 (Supplement to London Gazette P6582).

He left Newhaven in May 1915 to serve abroad. In the Supplementary to the London Gazette printed 22nd June 1915, P5976, Lieutenant Colonel Church is mentioned in despatches whilst on the General Headquarters Staff.

2. Lieutenant Colonel Cecil Alers Hankey, 3rd (Service Battalion), Royal Sussex Regiment 16th May 1915 to 20th August 1917.

The actual date that Lieutenant Colonel Hankey became Garrison Commander is not known. However, on 11th September 1916 he issued a public notice suspending the operation of Defence of the Realm (Consolidation) Regulations 1914, Regulation 29B relating to British Subjects resident in the Urban District of Newhaven and the parishes of Piddinghoe, Tarring Neville, Denton Urban, South Heighton and Bishopstone and their entry into the Newhaven Special Military Area.

On 1st March 1917 he issued a further public notice withdrawing the suspension. This was followed on 9th March 1917 by a public notice prohibiting the sale of .45 and .455 Calibre Pistols as Competent Military Authority of No. 5 Area, Eastern Command. See illustrations.

The 3rd Battalion, Royal Sussex Regiment's service digest contains the entry that "With effect from 1st June 1917 Lieutenant Colonel Hankey was appointed the Competent Military Authority with full powers under the Defence of the Realm Regulations for No. 11, Sussex Area, vice The Commandant, London Command Depot, Seaford (ref. E.C. Orders Nos. 99 dated 19th January 1917 and 352 dated 8th February 1917) ".

From 20th August 1917 to February 1918, however, Lieutenant Colonel Hankey served in France as Commanding Officer of the 2nd Battalion, Royal Sussex Regiment. During this time Major F.W.B. Willett D.S.O. was placed in temporary command of the 3rd Battalion. Lieutenant Colonel Hankey was back in command of the battalion in Newhaven by 31st March 1918.

3. Brigadier General Frederick Gore Anley C.B., C.M.G, April 1918 to December 1918

Brigadier General F.G. Anley was appointed GOC Newhaven Garrison from April to December 1918. He retired from the army on 19 October 1919. He was later County Director of the Sussex Branch of the Red Cross. He died in 1936 aged 72.

Defence of the Realm.

NEWHAVEN
SPECIAL MILITARY AREA

NOTICE IS HEREBY GIVEN that on and after the **FIFTEENTH DAY OF MARCH 1917**, the suspension of the operation of Defence of the Realm (Consolidation) Regulations 1914, Regulation 29B in so far as it affects persons of the description set forth in Clause 3 (i) of the Public Notice relating to the NEWHAVEN SPECIAL MILITARY AREA issued by me on the Eleventh day of September, 1916 will be WITHDRAWN.

Description of Persons Affected.

ANY PERSON being a **BRITISH SUBJECT** who was on the Twenty-second day of September 1916, **RESIDENT** in the Urban District of Newhaven and the Parishes of Piddinghoe, Tarring Neville, Denton Urban, South Heighton and Bishopstone.

Except as otherwise provided by the said Regulation or by Clause 3 (ii) of the aforesaid Public Notice, **NO PERSON** shall on or after the **FIFTEENTH DAY OF MARCH 1917**, enter the **NEWHAVEN SPECIAL MILITARY AREA** without permission from the Garrison Commander. Application for such permission should be made to the Garrison Commander at his Office in Newhaven. Permit Books containing forms of application and instructions as to the manner in which applications should be made may be obtained gratis from the Police and application for a Permit Book should be made to the Police Station nearest to the applicant's place of residence.

(Signed) **CECIL ALERS HANKEY, Lieut.-Colonel,**
Garrison Commander.
Commandant of the Newhaven Special Military Area
and Competent Military Authority.

Garrison Commander's Office,
Newhaven.

Dated this First day of March, 1917.

HODGSON, Printer, Newhaven and Seaford.

Defence of the Realm Regulations

SALE OF PISTOLS.

IN VIRTUE of the powers conferred on me by Regulation 30 of the Defence of the Realm (Consolidation) Regulations, 1914,

I, LIEUTENANT-COLONEL CECIL ALERS HANKEY, being a Competent Military Authority under the said Regulation, *do hereby direct and declare* that .45 and .455 Calibre *PISTOLS*, the property of licensed dealers, are **NOT TO BE SOLD.**

This Order to have effect from this date in the Urban District of Newhaven and the Parishes of Piddinghoe, Tarring Neville, Denton Urban, South Heighton, Denton and Bishopstone.

Given under my hand the 9th day of March, 1917.

(Signed) **C. A. HANKEY, Lieut.-Colonel,**
Garrison Commander,
Competent Military Authority,
No. 5 Area, Eastern Command.

NEWHAVEN.

HODGSON, Printer, Newhaven and Seaford.

NO. 1 DEPOT R.G.A.
FROM 5TH AUGUST 1914 TO 16TH MAY 1915

On mobilisation Major G.R.M. Church, Commanding the Depot, assumed the command of Newhaven Fortress (afterwards Garrison) with the temporary rank of Lieutenant Colonel. The command of the Depot devolved on Captain T.A. Whyte. Major J.T. Chapman, R.A. subsequently assumed command of the Depot on 16th November 1914 and lived with his wife Annie at 56 Fort Road, Newhaven with their 11 children. Captain D A Hosford, R.G.A was appointed Adjutant on 30th December 1914.

No. 1 Depot was one of the four main depots of the R.G.A. and quickly became, like the others, more of a reception depot for those newly enlisting, and later for those being conscripted or mobilised. Most of the Gunners would have only stayed between 2 to 4 weeks before being posted to companies, and later batteries being formed.

At 5.30 p.m. on the 5th August 1914 the order to mobilise was received and the Depot passed from Peace Establishment to War Establishment. A detachment of officers, N.C.O.s and men under Captain T.A. Whyte proceeded by the next train to Dover where the Mobilisation Store of the Depot was situated in order to prepare to equip about 770 reservists. It is believed that these reservists were recruited locally and probably included Newhaven men. This party arrived at Dover Castle at 11.45 p.m. on the 5th August and the work of dealing with the reservists commenced at 5 a.m. the following morning. On completion of this duty the party returned to Newhaven.

Great difficulty was experienced shortly afterwards in dealing with the abnormal influx of recruits owing to the paucity of officers and non-commissioned officers on the strength of the Depot at this time. Recruits arrived at the rate of between 150 and 200 daily, and on the 17th December 1914, the strength of the Depot reached a total of 3697 in Dover. Drafts varying from 50 to 700 were continually being despatched to various R.G.A. Commands. At this time men home from the Expeditionary Force were joining the Depot on the expiration of sick furlough and were subsequently posted to No. 2 Depot R.G.A. at Gosport.

Early in April 1915 recruiting for the duration of war recruits for the R.G.A. ceased and in consequence the Depot became less congested. Recruits were enlisted for 3 years or duration of war or one year for special reservists.

The No. 1 Depot R.G.A remained in Newhaven until 16th May 1915 when it was transferred to Fort Burgoyne, Dover.

The following No. 1 Depot Officers joined for duty on mobilisation:

Major J T Chapman, R.A.
Captain D A Hosford, R.G.A (Reserve of Officers)
Captain R H Manley, R.G.A. (Reserve of Officers)
Captain F J Robertson, R.A. (from retired pay)
CaptainL G Matterson, R.G.A
Captain (temporary) C A Vaux, R.G.A.
Lieutenant (temporary) G M Brew, R.G.A)
Second Lieutenant, afterwards Lieutenant G M Edwards, R.G.A.)
Second Lieutenant R C Mayne, R.G.A)
Second Lieutenant F G Prime, R.G.A.)
Second Lieutenant R G Clark, R.G.A.) On first
Second Lieutenant (temporary) J Long, R.G.A.) appointment
Second Lieutenant (temporary) F H Roberts, R.G.A.)
Second Lieutenant (temporary) D G Robinson, R.G.A.)
Second Lieutenant (temporary) P I Packington, R.G.A.)
Second Lieutenant (temporary) C L Arnold, R.G.A.)
Second Lieutenant A H J Toone, R.G.A.)
Second Lieutenant Anson E.A.
As time passed some officers left and were replaced.

When the Depot left Newhaven for Dover on 16th May 1915 their strength was 274 comprised of 4 officers, 95 N.C.O. s, 26 Depot Staff, 4 Trumpeters, 49 Boys and 96 Recruits.

Major J T. Chapman, Royal Artillery, Commanding Officer of No.1 Depot R.G.A

ROYAL DEFENCE CORPS

The men who served in the Royal Defence Corps were either too old or medically unfit for active front-line service. The role of the companies was to provide troops for security and guard duties inside the United Kingdom; guarding important locations such as ports or bridges.

The Royal Defence Corps furnished permanent guards on the following Vulnerable Points:

(i) Harbour Area ("North Quay" and "Wireless" Sections).
(ii) Trench Warfare Supply Depot, South Heighton Cement Works.
(iii) Glynde Reach Railway Bridge.
(iv) Southerham Railway Bridge.

And Examining Guards at the following entrances to the Newhaven Special Military Area:
(v) Town Station.
(vi) Seaford Road.
(vii) Lewes Road.
(viii) Brighton Road.

The 61st Protection Company and 102nd Protection Company of the Royal Defence Corps served in Newhaven as did a detachment of the 1st Home Service (H.S.) Garrison Battalion of the Buffs (East Kent Regiment). This battalion of the regiment was formed at Dover on 29th April 1916 as part of the Royal Defence Corps and in August 1917 it became 2nd Battalion Royal Defence Corps at Dover. The Home Service status indicated they were unable to be transferred overseas.

> 'The year 1916 emptied the crowded hutments [Meeching Rise camp] and it was a different Newhaven to which I eventually returned.
>
> There was no need of an officer's platoon and I passed whole lines of deserted huts. The guards which had provided us with so much strenuous employment

had been taken over by the Royal Defence Corps, that stout band of veterans who have never received their due. These worthies, many of them old men, quite unfit for camp conditions and sentry duty found innumerable guards on railway bridges, at power stations and other important places.

They suffered silently. Some of them died. One poor old fellow stepped out of the way of a train near Southerham Junction right into the path of a second train coming in the opposite direction. Another had his bayonet caught by a passing engine and was flung into the Ouse, where he was found next morning, frozen.'

Lieutenant G. D. Martineau, 3rd Battalion, Royal Sussex Regiment.

The Garrison strength return of 13th April 1917 showed that the, 61st Protection Company, Royal Defence Corps consisted of 2 officers and 57 men and that the detachment of the Buffs (East Kent Regiment) consisted of 2 officers and 275 men.

At some point the 61st Protection Company were replaced by a detachment of the 102nd Protection Company who had an approximate strength of 3 officers and 100 men in 1918.

12TH & 13TH (TRANSPORT WORKERS) BATTALIONS, BEDFORDSHIRE REGIMENT

The 12th and 13th (Transport Workers) Battalions were raised in December 1916 and March 1917 respectively and disbanded in August and December 1919 respectively. Their H.Q.'s were based in Croydon and, although dressed as infantry, they were never armed.

A detachment from these battalions was employed on transport work in Newhaven Harbour and was accommodated at the Railway Road Camp, in Newhaven.

In April 1917 it had 9 officers and 1062 men with an establishment of 9 officers and 1091 men. By 1918 its strength had diminished to 10 officers and 400 men.

29TH (WORKS) BATTALION, MIDDLESEX REGIMENT

A detachment of this regiment was in Newhaven in April 1917 when the Strength Return indicated that 1 officer and 178 men were present. However, it is not known what type of work on which they were employed.

Regimental details show that the battalion was formed in Mill Hill in July 1916. By March 1917 it had moved to Thetford, Norfolk and in April 1917 it was transferred to the Labour Corps as 5th Labour Battalion. It remained in the U.K. throughout the war.

53RD ANTI-AIRCRAFT COMPANY R.E.

This company appears in the 13th April 1917 Garrison Strength Return as having 2 officers and 25 men. An A.A. Company in the Royal Engineers manned searchlights.

It has been established that 4 Company London Electrical Engineers, R.E. manned the searchlight emplacements known to have existed near the Fort and harbour mouth but no information has been found about the men of the 53rd A.A. Company R.E. and their activities.

4TH BATTALION T.F., ROYAL SUSSEX REGIMENT
FROM 5TH AUGUST 1914 TO 24TH APRIL 1915

The 4th Battalion, Royal Sussex Regiment, was formed on 1st April 1908 under the Haldane Army Reforms and consisted of men from the old 2nd Volunteer Battalion and became part of the Territorial Force (T.F.). It recruited locally by companies as follows:

A Company	–	Haywards Heath and Uckfield
B Company	–	Hurst, Henfield, Steyning, Burgess Hill
C Company	–	East Grinstead, Crawley
D Company	–	Petworth and Midhurst
E Company	–	Horsham
F Company	–	Arundel and Storrington
G Company	–	Chichester and Bognor
H Company	–	Worthing.

At the outbreak of war these companies were brought together as one battalion and the 4th Battalion became Army Troops in the Home Counties Division T.F. (Territorial Force). They were based in Horsham on 4th August 1914.

The Battalion arrived in Newhaven on 5th August 1914. The Commanding Officer was Lieutenant-Colonel E.H.J.D. Mostyn.

The February 1913 Newhaven War Garrison Accommodation Plan showed that part of the 4th Battalion, 3 officers and 117 O.R.s. was to be accommodated in the Fort and this may well have happened.

An officer in the battalion, Major S W P Beale, maintained a diary during the time that the battalion was in Newhaven and this provides many details about the battalion and its activities.

DIARY OF MAJOR S.W.P. BEALE 4TH BATTALION, ROYAL SUSSEX REGIMENT

5th Aug 1914

After a long and tiring journey from Lark Hill Camp, Amesbury, Wiltshire the battalion arrived at Newhaven at 5.30 pm.

6th Aug 1914

'C', 'D', 'E', 'F' and 'G' Companies were detailed for fatigues; for the next two months continued and at the end of that time Newhaven had become in fact the Fortress that it was previously designed to be. The actual digging was done by civilian labour organised by Colonel Beris, our men put up barbed wire entanglements, cleared gorse bushes out of the field of fire, cut turf and used it to finish the head cover, filled and carried sand bags. There were besides many other lesser jobs but these were the principal ones.

7th Aug 1914

Lieutenant Hankey was appointed Fortress Transport Officer. A guard had been recruited by the Special Service Section from its arrival on July 30th on the Swing Bridge and the Pumping Station at Poverty Bottom, as well as on the Harbour Quays. From the first day of Mobilisation the battalion found guards (1) 2 officers and 60 men at the Inlying Picket and (2) 2 officers and 60 men at the Isolated Area, and the Company finding the latter had in addition to find 1 N.C.O and 6 men for the Bridge guard and 2 N.C.O. s and 9 men for the Railway Company's Pumping station at Denton.

8th Aug 1914

Captain Godman was detailed to perform the duty of visiting (by day and by night) the guards at the Fort, at the Breakwater and at Poverty Bottom. The guards were rearranged; one company now provided 2 officers and 60 men for Inlying Picket, 1 N.C.O. and 6 men for the Bridge, and 2 N.C.O. s and 9 men for Denton while the other company found 2 officers and 60 men which included the guard at Poverty Bottom.

9th Aug 1914

The Companies were paraded and shown their alarm posts.

10th Aug 1914
A return was called for of men willing to serve as Territorial Soldiers abroad.

14th Aug 1914
The North Wharf Area was added to the other guards.

15th Aug 1914
C.O. s parade on the Rec. (Recreation Ground) not a success.

24th Aug 1914
Second Lieutenant E Stephenson Clarke having joined was posted to 'D' Company.

25th Aug 1914
The Venerable Archdeacon Southwell was appointed chaplain to the defended post of Newhaven.

28th Aug 1914
The recruits that joined the battalion after the war began were at this time in some cases being dismissed from the square and becoming available for duty with their companies. As great difficulty had been experienced in finding the requisite numbers for guard they were badly wanted. 'E' Company were detailed to find every day 1 N.C.O and 9 men for guard on the footbridge over Mill Creek and 1 N.C.O and 14 men at the Isolated Area the strength of which was accordingly reduced.

30th Aug 1914
In preparation for musketry 2 N.C.O. s per Company were detailed for instruction and all available officers Colour Sergeants, Sergeants and Corporals were ordered to parade 12 -1 and 2.30 to 3.30 on the square.

31st Aug 1914
Second Lieutenant C H Campbell was promoted Lieutenant August 29th 1914. New alarm orders were issued.

1st Sep 1914
The first manoeuvres since Mobilisation was ordered for tomorrow. And the battalion being up to strength recruiting was stopped.

3rd Sep 1914

'F' Company moved from the Fortress R.E. Drill Hall to Station Road School and 'D' Company from H2 [map ref.] (below the Fort) to the Drill Hall.

4th Sep 1914

The M.G. Sections moved from 'E' Company (the Dock Labourers Waiting Room) to H2.

5th Sep 1914

Lieutenant Mostyn was detailed to supervise a recruit's course of musketry.

6th Sep 1914

Lieutenant S K Reid was transferred to 'B' Company and Second Lieutenant Weekes to 'F' Company.

7th Sep 1914

'C' Company was detailed for 3 days Company Training. Major-General J C Young Commanding Home Counties Division addressed the following letter to the C.O.:-

Canterbury 6th Sep 1914

'In a special order I congratulate the Division in the success of their concentration at Bordon and Longmoor and on the soldier like way in which the march to Salisbury Plain was carried out.

The subordination of physical discomfort to a high sense of discipline to which I alluded found a convincing illustration in the marching powers of the 2 battalions of the Royal Sussex Regiment and as Colonel of the regiment I look forward with confidence to their efficiently playing their part, if called upon, side by side with Regular Battalions'

Second Lieutenant C R H Weekes the first officer who actually joined the battalion after war began was dismissed drill on the square.

8th Sep 1914

O.C. (Officer Commanding) Companies were ordered to explain to the men the conditions of 'Imperial Service' and 'General Service' and a parade was ordered 'as strong as possible' on the following day when the C.O. called for those who volunteered for service abroad to fall out on the flank of the battalion. The numbers who responded were, officers 26, other ranks 731.

The Isolated Area guard was no longer found by 'E' Company in part, but reverted to the numbers of 2 officers and 60 other ranks.

11th Sep 1914

'B' Company were struck off other duties for 4 days Company Irayning (sic).

'H' Company were ordered to proceed to Shoreham and get a camp ready for the following day for the newly formed Division of what is usually called Kitchener's Army.

In consequence 'A' Company were moved to Hill Barn and found the men from the trenches etc in that post.

13th Sep 1914

The Engineers Fatigues were now beginning to come to an end and a programme of work for the following week was issued to the companies.

14th Sep 1914

'C' Company were detailed to proceed to Seaford to get ready a camp for the 22nd Service Division.

16th Sep 1914

Notice was given that recruits for the 4th (Reserve) Battalion would be enlisted and sent to Horsham.

17th Sep 1914

Captains Matthews and Kenderdine and Lieutenants Maples and C Campbell were detailed to proceed to Horsham for duty with the Reserve Battalion with Sergeants Spring and Stone and Lieutenant Campbell was ordered to relieve Lieutenant Frank who had been O.C. Depot.

21st Sep 1914

'H' Company returned from Shoreham and went into quarters at the Fort and the lines of tents were shifted lower down the hill and rather further from the road.

22nd Sep 1914

'A' Company moved from Hill Barn to the Casual Wards of the Workhouse.

There was still another rearrangement of the Guards, one company finding an officer, 7 N.C.O.s and 50 men, the other 1 officer 4 N.C.O. s and 50 men, while the Guard Commander was detailed in Battalion Orders.

The guard was directed to parade at the Goods Yard whence it would move off at the orders of the Guard Commander.

The Poverty Bottom Guard ceased to be visited by the Fortress Officer from this date which was a welcome relief.

The following extract from a letter received from the O.C. the camp at Shoreham was published with the C.O.'s congratulations to 'H' Company. 'They have had hard work, but it has been done with a thoroughness and alacrity that is beyond all praise'

Signed, H Bonham, Lieutenant Colonel, Camp Commandant, Shoreham Camp.

24th Sep 1914

Second Lieutenant E S Clarke joined on first appointment and was posted to 'D' Company.

1st Oct 1914

Imperial Service forms were issued to Companies for signature. These documents soon came to be known as 'death warrants'.

'C' Company returned from Seaford and, after pitching some more tents, were quartered on the Recreation Ground.

5th Oct 1914

C.S.S. J Wright was appointed Acting Sergeant Major, vice Acting Sergeant Major to Hook who relinquished the appointment at his own request. Acting Sergeant Major Hook was transferred to the Depot dated October 10th.

8th Oct 1914

The Boundaries of the Fortress were extended roughly to the line of the entanglements on the W(est) of the Base and on the E (ast) to include Denton, Norton, Bishopstone and Blatchington Coast Guard Station. Considerable inconvenience had been caused by the previous narrow bounds which were in fact only the town of Newhaven.

The numbers for guard were reduced, for the Company finding the Isolated Area from 50 to 30 men and for the Inlying Picket from 7 to 5 N.C.O.s Lieutenant R J B Frank took over the duties of Fortress Transport Officer.

9th Oct 1914

The Adjutant produced the first lecture of the season on 'maps'

10th Oct 1914

The Army Order dealing with proficiency pay was published; in effect that an N.C.O. or man must have attended 2 fifteen day camps before mobilization in order to get it. The usual number of hard cases was immediately found to exist.

11th Oct 1914

Training in trench digging began this week.

13th Oct 1914

Notice was given that on the division of the Battalion into 'Imperial Service' and 'House Service' units the promotion of N.C.O.s would be from a general roll.

14th Oct 1914

Second Lieutenant Ridley was selected as Scout Officer with Corporal Wyatt as Scout Sergeant.

19th Oct 1914

Lieutenant E H Mostyn was appointed Assistant Adjutant

21st Oct 1914

To the regret of the officers the Allowance in lieu of rations was reduced from 2/- to 1/9d a day, but

22nd Oct 1914

At a meeting of the mess a report was presented of a committee Major Campion, the Archdeacon of Lewes and Lieutenant Duffield Jones, which had been appointed by the C.O. to investigate the cost of the mess. It was to the effect that the cost should be reduced to 5/6d a day.

At the same meeting a proposal was put forward that this Battalion should send a present to the 2nd Battalion, and a committee was appointed to carry out the proposition.

The N.C.O.s of the Battalion were put into seniority roll and allotted from that roll to Companies in rotation. This move caused considerable discussion and quite a number of prophecies of the gloomiest description. Later on even the prophets became more or less reconciled.

Colour Sergeant W F Wraight was commissioned as Lieutenant and Q.M. to the Battalion and Lance Sergeant Churcher took his place as O.R. (sic) Sergeant.

A small number of sergeants were transferred to the Depot at Horsham.

24th Oct 1914

The following were gazetted:

To be Captains (Temporary); E W Bennett (late Captain of the Battalion) and E T Hodgson (Late Lieutenant, 2nd Vol. Battalion, the Royal Sussex Regiment.) To be Second Lieutenants; T M Davies, C F L St George, C E Lucas, A H Bennett, J M Borrer

Of the above Captain E T Hodgson was attached to 'B' Company and T Davies to 'H' Company.

25th Oct 1914

For the present the O.C. the 4th (Reserve) Battalion, Royal Sussex Regiment will also command the Depot at Horsham.

26th Oct 1914

'E' Company moved from the Fortress R.E. Drill Hall to the Dock Labourers Waiting Room at the Harbour Station.

The training of the Battalion had now reached the stage when a Battalion tactical exercise could take place. It did now.

29th Oct 1914

Colour Sergeant Instructor Nye was appointed Acting Sergeant Major of the 4th

(Reserve) Battalion and Q.M. Sergeant Corden and Colour Sergeants Cullen and Keates were ordered to Horsham for duty with the Reserve Battalion. As a result the following were promoted: - Colour Sergeant Flint, Q.M. Sergeant, Colour. Sergeant Ins(tructor) Jones temporary Colour Sergeant To 'G' Company, Colour Sergeant Ins (tructor) Bamber temporary Colour Sergeant to 'C' Company, Sergeant Seagrave Colour Sergeant to 'E' Company.

30th Oct 1914

125 Imperial Service Recruits arrived from Horsham and were formed into a company under command of Lieutenant A N H Weekes.

Second Lieutenant V Richardson was gazetted to the Battalion and Captain W H Kenderdine and Second Lieutenant Maples were transferred to the Depot while Captain H E Matthews and Lieutenant C H Campbell were transferred to the Reserve Battalion.

The following notices from the Gazette were also published today:

R F Mitchell (Temporary Captain)

W H Fribe (Temporary Captain)

W F Campbell (Temporary Lieutenant)

A C Rowden (Temporary Lieutenant)

H G Messel (Temporary Lieutenant)

J de V Loder (Second Lieutenant)

F Goring (Second Lieutenant)

and officers at Newhaven were posted:

Captains Hodgson and Bennett and Second Lieutenant Middleton to 'B' Company.

Second Lieutenants Loder and Davies to 'H' Company

Second Lieutenants Bennett and Borrer to 'C' Company.

1st Nov 1914

Extract from the *Gazette*:

R C S Middleton to be Second Lieutenant

The first notice was taken of the 1914 Infantry Training. We left off forming fours according to the old book.

2nd Nov 1914

Second Lieutenant C F L St George was attached to 'D' Company and Second Lieutenant F Goring to 'F'.

The Battalion had its dinners 'cooked out'.

4th Nov 1914

From the *Gazette*:

Second Lieutenant D N Tyrrell Green to be Second Lieutenant [confirmed as]

At battalion training the flag system as described in a recent issue of the Army Review was tried.

6th Nov 1914

Lieutenant and Q.M. W F Wraight took over from Captain and Hon. Maj. W H Loninge (?) who was transferred to the Reserve Battalion.

Second Lieutenants D N Tyrrell Green, V Richardson and Lieutenant H Messell were attached respectively to 'F', 'G' and 'D' Companies.

About this time the need for more clothing became pressing. August, September and October had been on the whole hot and dry. November began with a good deal of rain and then there came some early frosts.

On mobilization the clothing of the Battalion was nearly time expired and it had been severely tried, first by the wet days on the march at the end of the training period and afterwards by the continuous rough work on Engineers Fatigues and later by the work (equally hard for uniform) of Company and Battalion Training. There were numbers of the men whose clothing was in rags and boots were in holes.

8th Nov 1914

From the Gazette: Major R M Helme to be Lieutenant Colonel (Temporary)

9th Nov 1914

Rations were taken and cooked 'out' in mess tins.

Lieutenant Colonel Helme, Maj. Hodgson and Lieutenant Hankey were detailed to go to Horsham for duty with the Reserve Battalion. Maj. Hodgson handed over command of the E (East) defences to Captain Beale. Major Campion continued to look after the W (West) defences.

12th Nov 1914

Five more N.C.O. s was transferred to the Reserve Battalion.

'F' Company moved from the schools in Station Road to huts which had been erected on ground adjoining.

18th Nov 1914

Second Lieutenant Middleton was appointed Signalling Officer.

21st Nov 1914

The officers at headquarters with a few hardy exceptions moved out of tents to the next huts to be finished which happened to be at the top of the second row from the west.

Late last night the 'alarm' was blown. The new searchlight in the Fort fixed itself firmly on a hostile airship which moved slowly with the wind and showed, at intervals, what might have been a light. We doubled and fell in (and fell down) and borrowed other people's rifles. Then we all waited for orders which seemed slow in coming. Then we were told to dismiss and went (or went back) to bed. There was an attempt at a second alarm but it didn't go very far.

22nd Nov 1914

We had another 'alarm' between tea and dinner. This one didn't last very long and seems to have originated in some enthusiastic Boy Scout buglers who were practising. We begin to know what to do fairly well.

29th Nov 1914

The following promotions were published:

Captain and Hon. Major W R Campion and Captain S W P Beale to be Majors with effect from 12th Nov 1914.

Lieutenants E A Duffield Jones, A N H Weekes, J E H Mostyn , H T S Gray to be Captains- the first two 17th Sep the others 12 Nov 14 and

Second Lieutenants M Medlycott, R E Loder, E R Campbell, R J B Frank and W O'B G Frank to be Lieutenants – the first two 17th Sep the rest 12th Nov 1914.

Officers were posted:

'A' Company Captain Warren, Lieutenants Reid and Worsley.

'B' Company Captain Weekes , Lieutenant R Frank, and Lieutenant F Goring (Second Lieutenant Richardson attached).
'C' Company Captain Mostyn, Lieutenant E R Campbell, Second Lieutenant Ridley,
'D' Company Captain B Constable, Lieutenant Messel, Second Lieutenant Clarke.
'E' Company Captain Godman, Lieutenant Loder (M.G) and W O'B G Frank , Second Lieutenant Jebb.
'F' Company Captain G Constable, Second Lieutenants Weekes and Maxwell Stuart
'G' Company Capt Duffield Jones, Lieutenant Medleycott, Second Lieutenant Tyrell Green.
'H' Company Captain Gray, Second Lieutenants Middleton and Loder (and Davies attached)

The Battalion began to practise digging trenches at this time.

The following officers were detailed to proceed to Horsham for duty with the Reserve Battalion: Captains Bennett and Hodgson, Second Lieutenants Borrer, Davis and Richardson.

1st Dec 1914

Captains Bennett and E T Hodgson were detailed to proceed to Horsham tomorrow.

2nd Dec 1914

An Army Order was published dealing with Separation Allowances and Ration Allowances.

10th Dec 1914

Now that four companies ('B', 'C', 'D' and 'H') had got into the huts at Headquarters and the weather continued wet, the wind began to get past a joke and we started making paths, nearly all of which were successful in the end.

13th Dec 1914

127 Home Service men were ordered to Horsham.

16th Dec 1914

The numbers for guard were reduced to 48 and 52 men respectively from the two companies finding the duty.

21st Dec 1914
The Headquarter companies were provided with an Orderly Officer after this.

25th Dec 1914
Christmas Day was celebrated by all the companies except 'C' and 'D' (for guard), with a dinner at which the C.O. made a speech.

26th Dec 1914
'C' and 'D' Companies fed.

27th Dec 1914
Lieutenants Reid and Campbell and Second Lieutenants Jebb and J Loder were detailed to go to Hythe for a Musketry Course and Lieutenant R Loder and L/Sgt Aries for a M.G. Course.

28th Dec 1914
The Recruit Company completed their Musketry Course.

30th Dec 1914
The Annual Course of Musketry was begun.

1st Jan 1915
Everybody without exception was aware of the New Year arrival last night, however fast asleep he had been earlier. The steamers in the harbour blew their whistles and rang their bells with tremendous vigour. Some of us took it for the 'alarm', but not seriously enough to leave our blankets.

An N.C.O. s class was warned for instruction in the Gymnasium.

2nd Jan 1915
We were warned that the huts were to be match-boarded inside, an improvement that we all thought was overdue. Soup in the evening was instituted for the Headquarter Companies.

About this time the Battalion began to suffer rather severely from influenza.

7th Jan 1915
Second Lieutenant E S Clarke was appointed Regimental Transport Officer but

he went on sick leave in the afternoon.

9th Jan 1915
The latest batch of recruits was warned to begin musketry.

11th Jan 1915
We got some nice (!!) new alarm orders in case we get bombarded from the sea or bombed from the air.

12th Jan 1915
As a sort of celebration of the return of our party from Hythe, Second Lieutenant Jebb lectured on 'Musketry'.

18th Jan 1915
We began to practise digging trenches at night.

Second Lieutenants Jebb and C R H Weekes were warned to go to Hythe for M.G. (Machine Gun) and Musketry courses respectively.

20th Jan 1915

Owing to the shortage of men for guards due to influenza the signaller scouts and M.G. Section took a turn.

We were warned of the coming of the 4 Company Organization and the companies were allotted to their new designations and stations:

'A' and 'H' became 'A' Company at Headquarters
'B' and 'D' became 'B' Company at the Workhouse
'C' and 'E' became 'C' Company at Headquarters
'F' and 'G' became 'D' Company at Railway Road and the Custom House.
Officers were posted:-
'A' Company – Major Beale, Captain Warren, Captain Gray. No. 1 Platoon Lieutenant Reid, No.2 Lieutenant Worsley, No.3 Second Lieutenant Middleton, No. 4 Second Lieutenant J Loder
'B' Company – Captain B Constable , Captain A Weekes, No. 5 Platoon Lieutenant Messel, No. 6 Lieutenant R Frank, No. 7 Second Lieutenant F Goring, No. 8 Second Lieutenant St George
'C' Company – Captain Godman, Captain Mostyn, Lieutenant R E Loder

(M.G.), No. 9 Platoon Lieutenant E R Campbell, No. 10 Lieutenant W Frank, No. 11 Second Lieutenant Ridley, No. 12 Second Lieutenant Jebb
'D' Company – Captain G Constable, Captain Duffield Jones, No. 13 Platoon Lieutenant Medlycott, No. 14 Second Lieutenant Weekes, No. 15 Second Lieutenant Tyrrell Green, No 16 Second Lieutenant Maxwell Stuart

The following appointments were also made:
'A' Company C.S.M. Colour Sergeant A Agate C.Q.M.S Colour Sergeant G Baker
'B' Company C.S.M. Colour Sergeant E Mitchell C.Q.M.S Colour Sergeant Bray
'C' Company C.S.M. Colour Sergeant F Seagrave C.Q.M.S Colour Sergeant Bamber
'D' Company C.S.M. Colour Sergeant A Swain C.Q.M.S Colour Sergeant A Jones
Second Lieutenant E S Clarke was gazetted to the Scots Guards.

21st Jan 1915
The Brighton Road and Lewes Road guards were discontinued and a 'one sentry' guard was established at the Conservative Club at the top of the High Street so that the numbers for guard (found by our company) were reduced to 3 officers, 9 N.C.O. s and 97 men.

We were told to say 'Garrison' instead of 'Fortress'.

22nd Jan 1915
We received orders that we had been selected for 'Service on the Continent' and heard that we were entitled to 3 days leave, all round in consequence both of which announcements caused general rejoicings.

The Adjutant was in the Gazette promoted Captain in this regiment.

25th Jan 1915
'B' Company began the merry game of fitting clothes etc. to go foreign.

27th Jan 1915
A second recruit company, 123 strong, came in from Horsham. Lieutenant Reid

and Second Lieutenant J Loder were told off to them.

In view of the probability of active service in the immediate future men who had not signed on for Imperial Service were urged to do so and all ranks were warned to get inoculated.

29th Jan 1915

Among quantities of stores of all description there arrived 30 sets of web equipment for the officers.

31st Jan 1915

'D' Company began the return of rifles and drawing new, sighted for Mark VII ammunition.

The Recruit Company was isolated as one of them got spotted fever.

1st Feb 1915

The Quartermaster ricked his back badly and Captain Gray acted for him while he was in hospital.

2nd Feb 1915

An order was published thanking the Archdeacon of Lewes for his work here and wishing him luck abroad.

All the last few days there had been occasional cases of measles – the proportion among the officers being much heavier than in the other ranks.

An officer's mess meeting was held at which the arrangements for foreign service was discussed.

5th Feb 1915

Sergeant E C Churcher was discharged on appointment to a commission in the R.F.A.

9th Feb 1915

The fitting out got down to boots.

13th Feb 1915

The 3 days leave was enjoyed by everyone in turn - the home service men last.

When they came back they were sorted out and sent to Horsham today.

18th Feb 1915

The Battalion was inspected by the Lord Lieutenant of the County in fullest war paint. The Hon. Colonel the Duke and the C.O. all made speeches

It is hoped that Captain C R B Godman's horse will have a fortnight on the square to learn drill.

The Battalion, in fact, drilled better than it has done before.

20th Feb 1915

There appeared some new orders about shooting at aircraft.

An attempt was made to keep the non-contacts with the measles apart from the contacts. It didn't last very long.

24th Feb 1915

We were notified that the Battalion would not be required at present for service on the continent. Rumours were even quicker than usual in exaggerating the force of the blow. We were all disappointed.

26th Feb 1915

The two Captain Constables fought a battle (sic).

8th March 1915

The lights were downed for the second time.

10th March 1915

The Officers played the Sergeants at footer on the rec. The Sergeants won after a clash.

16th March 1915

An essential step in getting ourselves clear of measles was taken. The blankets were disinfected in batches of 200.

19th Mar 1915

We got new straw for the palliasses and bolsters.

20th Mar 1915
Second Lieutenant Ridley came back from and Second Lieutenant St George went to, Hythe to take a Division at Cambridge and Captain Mostyn and the Q.M. were warned to take an advance party tomorrow to sort things there

Second Lieutenant A W Butler and Second Lieutenant F B Briggs joined from Horsham (the former with a draft of 60 men) and were posted to 'D' and 'A' Companies respectively and Second Lieutenant Tyrell Green was transferred from 'D' to 'A'.

Maj. W R Campion was gazetted Lieutenant Colonel

The following order was published:

> 'The C.O. on handing over the command to Maj. Campion cannot allow the regiment to leave for active service without bidding all ranks a most affectionate farewell and wishing them every good luck. It is to him a very sad farewell – to be forced to leave the regiment when the summit of his ambition had been reached but he looks forward to the time, which he trusts is not far distant when he may be allowed once again to resume the command of the Battalion.
>
> The discipline, good behaviour and cheerful way all ranks have done their duty during a very trying winter has won his highest admiration and appreciation, and the loyal and untiring way in which all have assisted him in the training of the Battalion enables him to hand it over in a state of high efficiency and he feels certain that all will extend to their new Commanding Officer in a task of the greatest responsibility the same loyal and affectionate support which he has ever received, and he feels confident that the Regiment will uphold the highest tradition of the Royal Sussex Regiment.
>
> Farewell and his fervent prayer will be that God will bless and prosper the old Regiment.'

1st April 1915
4 N.C.O. s per company started a week's course of Range taking.

3rd April 1915
Sir Edmund Loder sent us two miniature rifles per company and a quantity of ammunition.

Also the Battalion was reported free from measles and our hopes for a change revived.

Lieutenant H Messel was granted leave on medical certificate and is apparently not going to rejoin for some time.

6th April 1915

The 9th Battalion sent a footer team over to play us and got beaten, a proposal that both battalions should march to Rottingdean and play a return didn't come off.

We got news that a 3rd Line 4th Battalion is being raised to consist of foreign service men only with an establishment of 60%. On referring to an Army Order we comforted ourselves with the reflection that the 3rd Line Unit, in cases where the 1st Line one is not for foreign, has an establishment of 25%.

10th April 1915

The Corporals room was opened for use.

Second Lieutenant Goring got sick leave which seems likely to be extended for some time.

14th April 1915

Captain Duffield Jones was transferred to Horsham and Captain Warren from 'A' was posted to 'D' Company. Captain Gray was restored to the establishment and posted to 'A' Company.

15th April 1915

'B' Company vacated the Workhouse and moved into the depot huts and the Transport shifted from Denton and other places to the 'Valley Camp'.

16th April 1915

Yesterday we had to find parties for a road blocking scheme. The Inlying picket had a job and parties were detailed for Southease Bridge and the Brighton Road at Rottingdean. Their bag didn't amount to much. It happened again tonight.

18th April 1915

The Battalion was ordered to be in readiness to move.

19th April 1915
Lieutenant W G Bridger and Second Lieutenant R P Young joined from Horsham and were posted to 'B' Company.

20th April 1915
Three Battalions from Seaford came up against us in the night. We tried to hold Denton and the G.O.C. said we didn't know the ground. The invaders took the trench on the beach (according to the umpire) but were adjudged losers on points – or time.

21st April 1915
The G.O.C. told us yesterday that we were to shift on Thursday (tomorrow) but at the mess a wire arrived postponing the move to Saturday 24th.

22nd April 1915
The latest is that we join the Welsh.

24th April 1915
Two companies of the 2nd/4th Battalion arrived before 9.00 am and our first trainload paraded at 9.30 and went off at 10.15, the second following at 12. Lieutenant Colonel Mostyn in each case called the parade to attention and then saw them off from the station as did the Garrison Commander and all the Transport Staff and other friends from Newhaven. In fact the whole town turned out twice.

The 4th Battalion left Newhaven on 24th April 1915 as it had been posted to the 160th Brigade, 53rd (Welsh) Division in Cambridge.

NOTE: In May 1915 the 4th battalion became 1st/4th and 2nd/4th and 3rd/4th were formed later on. The 1st/4th Battalion subsequently went to Gallipoli leaving Devonport on 17th July 1915 and arriving in Egypt on 28th July 1915. They landed at Suvla Bay on the Gallipoli Peninsular on 9th August 1915 when the Battalion was about 750 strong. On the 10th August after going into action the Battalion War Diary put their strength as 250 men.

Major Beale went on to take command of the battalion on 26th May 1917. The Battalion went to France in May 1918.

Major S.W.P. Beale, 4th Battalion, Royal Sussex Regiment in 1914 [WSR]

4th Battalion, Royal Sussex Regiment on parade on Newhaven Recreation Ground prior to leaving for Cambridge 24th April 1915.[WSR

3RD (RESERVE) BATTALION, ROYAL SUSSEX REGIMENT
FROM 16TH MAY 1915 TO THE END OF THE WAR

The 3rd (Reserve) Battalion, Royal Sussex was based in Chichester at the outbreak of the war. On mobilisation it moved to Dover and on 16th May 1915 it moved to Newhaven for duty as Newhaven Garrison where it was accommodated at the Meeching Rise Camp.

The battalion acted as a feeder battalion, training and furnishing drafts to the regular battalions while at the same time guarding the coastal area around Newhaven. It was also intended that the 3rd (Reserve) Battalion of a regiment would absorb the immature and unfit from the line battalions as well. Captain R. Church, 12th Hampshire Regiment had joined the battalion on 13th May 1915 as 'Draft Conducting Officer'.

Lieutenant Colonel Cecil Alers Hankey was the Commanding Officer of the battalion throughout the war except between 20th August 1917 and February 1918 when he served in France as Commanding Officer of the 2nd Battalion, Royal Sussex Regiment. During this time Major F.W.B. Willett D.S.O. was placed in temporary command of the 3rd Battalion. Lieutenant-Colonel Hankey was back in command of the battalion in Newhaven by 31st March 1918 and had been granted an extension in command of the battalion until 23rd April 1919.

An officer of the 3rd (Reserve) Battalion wrote of his experiences during his time in Newhaven:

> 'Above the orderly room where I reported rose the Fort-then commanded by an uncle of mine. North of the Fort, the coastal ridge sloped down to the recreation ground, where we paraded and on the other side of this was Meeching Rise. The 3rd Battalion was encamped on both these eminences-first in tents and later in lines and lines of wooden huts, approached over duckboards through clinging mud.

I think there must have been over a hundred officers and something like 2,000 men with the Reserve Battalion, "united", as the papers put it, "in a common and righteous cause.

The point on which we were more evidently united was a dislike of Newhaven, and it was often referred to as "New Hades". We lived within a belt of barbed wire and had to obtain leave to go outside this limit. Brighton, which did not attract me, appeared to us a "demi-Paradise", and we escaped there whenever we could, returning either by bus along the perilously darkened coast road or by late train, changing at Lewes.

The bus once stopped for some time at Telscombe Cliffs, in order to enable the conductor to have a fight with one of the passengers who lived there. I sought the combatants, found them smiting the darkness with vicious intention, and ordered the conductor back to his bus, as though I had been a policeman. I also took the civilian's address and scared him into his house and we got back safely.

The train journey was a weary business and sometimes, overcome by sleep, I was taken on to Seaford. This circumstance could be met by taking the docker's train back to Newhaven at 1 a.m. The latter train was unsavoury enough to be known as "Lousy Lou" and a judicious tip opened the way to the comparative luxury of the guard's van.

Nearly all of us were longing to go out to France. Some more thoughtful men may have been less eager, and those who had already been were not disposed to share our enthusiasm, but most of us were too young to see much further than our noses.

Meanwhile Colonel Hankey and the Adjutant Captain Ashworth, must have wondered what to do with the surplus officers.

The great massacre of the Somme was yet to come [1st July 1916] and here were subalterns crowding the barrack square, till some wag described a platoon as "a body of men surrounded by officers".

R.S.M Boniface nearly broke his heart over us and Sergeant "Patsy" Short, in peace time a balloon-seller on Eastbourne front, would take us up a pleasant valley, where, after a little instruction, we would exchange anecdotes, until the Adjutant's appearance brought "Patsy" to his feet with the remark:

"Now then gentlemen. 'Ere 'e comes! Stop talking, now, please. I gets all the blame".

He was very exact in pacing out distances on parade- a method he adopted later in the German offensive of 1918, when all his officers were knocked out. His action restored confidence, and gained him the M.M. [Military Medal].

Finally, an officer's platoon was formed, which marched about and carried out training on its own account.

Guard duties absorbed a fair proportion of the men, and the orderly officer had to do a tremendous round. The 3rd Royal Sussex found guards so far apart as Bishopstone, Barn Hill, Denton Waterworks and the Cement Works at Heighton, where there was a huge store of explosives. A sentry was even posted at the end of the stone jetty or breakwater, and had to be inspected after 11 pm. I do not remember whether he was supposed to challenge submarines, but in the end a man was washed over by a heavy sea and drowned.

One of the duties of the orderly officer was to test telephones and ask to be put through to the fort.

A sergeant in charge of one guard was on familiar terms with the girl at the exchange and when I took up the receiver, a cheerful voice said:

"Hullo, George!"

I cleared my throat and said sternly:

"I want the fort, please".

"You don't want much, George", came the easy reply, as she put me through.

There were officers' guards on the town station and the harbour, the former having charge of a key which could plunge the whole of Newhaven into merciful darkness. It was profoundly stirring to get a message that there were seven Zeppelins over Dieppe, and it gave one a sense of power to turn the key and watch the lights die out in town and camp. It was less uplifting to learn that one had taken this action in the middle up the Colonel's best no-trumper.

Actually, Newhaven was never raided. Why I cannot think, since it was a most important port for the sending of food supplies and munitions to France. The Downs over Bishopston[e] and Norton held anti-aircraft guns, and raids were always anticipated.

There were German spy scares and lights were reported in the marshes and on the hills with an answering flash from the sea when a destroyer went out in the evening.

Also, there were "periods of vigilance", when all leave was stopped and we were informed that the Germans had laid plans to land demolition parties from disguised trawlers. To counter this, the authorities organised officers' patrols, six strong, to watch the beach from Newhaven to Seaford. I have done that patrol in a blizzard, and once walked almost on to the revolver of an ill-tempered subaltern of the Border Regiment, who carried on the good work on the Seaford front.

When this "vigilance" was relaxed the leave-book was crowded with names, and we sped to Brighton with money in our pockets and gaiety in our hearts.

One of my brother officers was a tall, thin Etonian, unsoldierly in appearance but with a quaint humour, which appealed to me. He invited me to dinner at a most expensive hotel, and addressed some remarks to the head waiter in a strange tongue. The man seemed taken aback, but wrote down the order and retired.

Various people were staring at us.

"What was all that?" I enquired. My host smiled.

"Oh," he said, "there are so many German Jews sitting about here and talking English that it always amuses me to come and order my dinner in German".

One officer, not from Newhaven, was most unfortunate at the same hotel. Excited by liquor, he jumped on to a chair in the crowded lounge, and shouted: "To your tents, O Israel!"

Sensitiveness led to action and inquiry. His condition was revealed and he was court-martialled and cashiered.

The time of waiting came to an end soon enough.

We knew well the stirring notes of the "Roussillon" march and the free lilt of "Sussex by the Sea". We knew also the newer airs which the men of the drafts always sang- "Keep the Home Fires Burning" and "Pack up your Troubles". I wish people would not try to revive these last two songs; they lose their meaning when they are sung by a generation which cannot comprehend.

On the town station the band played "Auld Lang Syne", and the women cried openly. The year 1916 emptied the crowded hutments and it was a different Newhaven to which I eventually returned.

I love the Downs behind Seaford and particularly the little hamlets of Bishopston[e] and Norton. I can even cross the valley and look with pleasure on Piddinghoe's "begilded dolphin". But the harbour town I pass swiftly and do not check my pace as I go over the hill, for there, where once we "advanced in short

> rushes from the left" and observed the enemy "two fingers four o'clock of the haystack", Newhaven has found its perfect foster-brother".

Throughout the war there was a constant flow of officers and O.R. s into the battalion and out to other regiments and other battalions of the Royal Sussex Regiment. Drafts were regularly leaving for service to the B.E.F. in France, Egypt, India, and, later, Italy, as well as other units in the UK. For example, on 11th October 1915 35 men were sent to Seaford to join the 1st (Garrison) Battalion, the Norfolk Regiment and on 8th November 1915 200 men were sent to the Hampshire Regiment at Gosport. The 2nd, 7th and 9th battalions of the Royal Sussex Regiment received regular drafts from Newhaven. These included machine gunners and signallers.

On 30th September 1915 a portion of the battalion took part in a 'Recruitment Rally' at Eastbourne.

The following telegram was published in orders for the 3rd Battalion in early June 1916:

> *"His Majesty The King commands that all officers of the Army shall wear mourning with their uniforms for a period of one week, commencing 7th June, on the melancholy occasion of the death of the late Field Marshall Right Honourable Earl Kitchener of Khartoum".*

Lord Kitchener had been killed on 5th June 1916 when the warship, H.M.S. Hampshire, taking him on a diplomatic mission to Russia, struck a mine and sank west of the Orkney Islands. A number of Newhaven men are known to have been on this ship.

Captain W.H.W. Apperley was appointed Physical and Training Supervising officer to the troops stationed at Newhaven and Shoreham on 7th June 1916.

A memorial service was held on 13th June 1916 in Christ Church, Newhaven for the late Lord Kitchener [Christ Church was demolished in 1965 and Newhaven Police Station now occupies the site at junction of South Way with South Road].

The demand for men became such that drafts of untrained and partially trained men were despatched to France. On 3rd September 1916, for example, 200 untrained men were drafted and on 4th June 1917 42 trained and 24 partially trained men were drafted.

The Daily Strength Return of 3rd Battalion on 13th April 1917 showed that 82 officers and 1393 O.R.'s were present out of an authorised establishment of 146 and 1807 respectively. By 1918 the authorised establishment had reduced to 40 officers and 1553 men.

At the end of 1917 the Adjutant of the 3rd Battalion reported that since the war began a total of 474 officers and 11,519 O.R.s had been drafted.

Letters and postcards from his family meant a great deal to the serving soldier.

The wife of Private Harold Carver, G/12223, 3rd Battalion, Royal Sussex Regiment used a code to disguise the message on the postcard that she sent to her husband in Newhaven Camp in August 1916. However, the main content of the message can be determined by moving the last letter on each written word to be the first letter of that word resulting in the message reading as:

> "Here I am darling back home again after seeing you angel hubby off. I hope you will have a good journey you had plenty of friends & looked quite happy but oh how I miss you precious now. Come back to me soon won't you darling. I am thinking of you always dearest & may God bless you and keep you...."

Private Carver was transferred to the Middlesex Regiment being re-assigned the service number G/40307 and from there to the 8th Battalion, the London Regiment (Post Office Rifles) again being re-assigned a new service no of 388273.

The 8th Battalion, the London Regiment had landed in France on 18th March 1915. Harold joined this regiment in France at some date after 13th August 1916, the post mark date on the card. He probably survived the war as he is not mentioned in the C.W.G.C. list of casualties.

Private Carver was awarded the British War and Victory medals.

I'm feeling so lonely
without you
The hours all too slowly
pass by
The days seem so long now
you're absent
When you're here all too
quickly they fly
But I think of and pray
for you always
And remember the past
happy time
And look forward with joy
to our meeting
Which will once more
make life seem divine

12223 Private H Carver, 17 Platoon, 3rd Royal Sussex, 5th Company, E. 6 Hut, Meeching Rise Camp, Newhaven, Sussex [NFA]

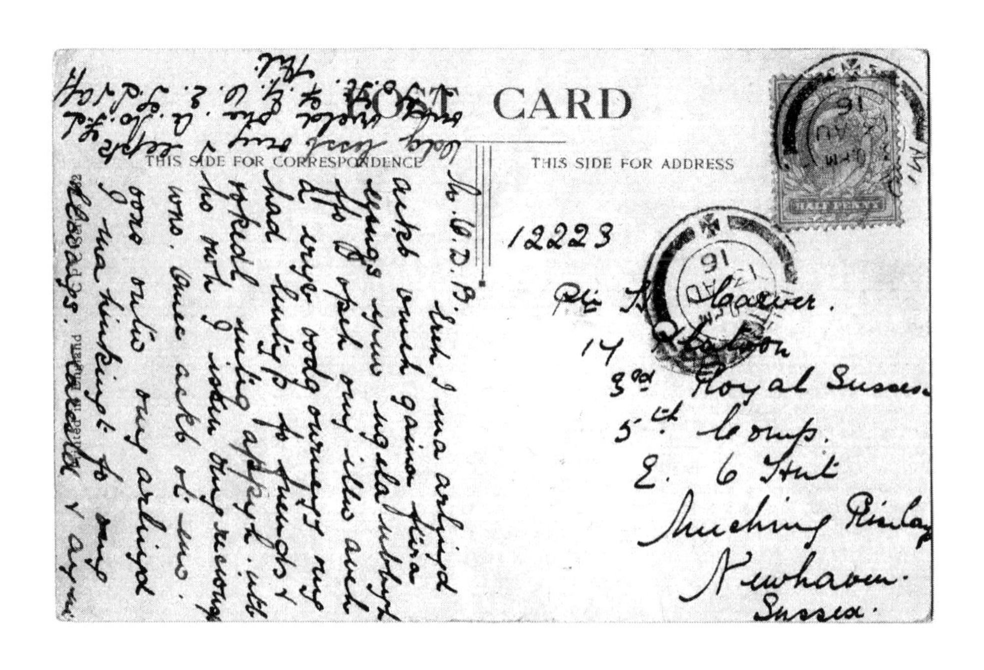

Troops on parade on the parade ground, what is now the recreation ground Court Farm Road, Newhaven shown below in 2014 [NFA]

SECOND LIEUTENANT JOHN BOLAS LANE, 3RD BATTALION, ROYAL SUSSEX REGIMENT

The Digest of the 3rd Battalion, Royal Sussex Regiment, records that a General Court Martial assembled at Newhaven on Wednesday 10th November 1915 at 11 a.m. for the trial of Second Lieutenant John Bolas Lane of the regiment.

President:
  Colonel C.H. Hitchins, 10th Border Regiment.
Members:
  Major A.J. Martineau, 1/1st Company Sussex R.G.A.
  Major L.A. Sherrard, Royal Engineers.
  Major W.A. Dow, 2/1st Comapany, Sussex R.G.A.
  Major A.E. Levin, No. 4 Company, London Electrical Engineers.
  Captain A.J. Parkin, 3rd Battalion, Royal Sussex Regiment.
  Captain A.W.K.Lloyd, Battalion, Royal Sussex Regiment.
  Captain W.F. Grinsted, 1/1st Company, Sussex R.G.A.
  Captain T.H. Vitty, No. 4 Company, London Electrical Engineers.
  Captain L. St. P. Beynon, 3rd Battalion, Royal Sussex Regiment.
  Captain C. de St. Croix, 3rd Battalion, Royal Sussex Regiment.
Waiting Members:
  Captain L.L. Boyne, 3rd Battalion, Royal Sussex Regiment.
Judge Advocate:
  Major W. Appleyard, 3rd Battalion, Royal Sussex Regiment.

Lieutenant A.C. Clayton, 2nd Battalion, Royal Sussex Regiment prosecuted. The trial lasted two days. The Court found the accused guilty of the charge on which he was arraigned and sentenced him to be 'Severely Reprimanded'.

This was duly confirmed by his majesty King George V and was promulgated by Lieutenant Colonel Hankey on 26th November 1915 at Newhaven.

Who was Second Lieutenant Lane? On what charge was he arraigned? What happened to him?

John Bolas Lane was born in Chiswick, Middlesex on 25th July 1882. His parents were William Henry Lane and Ann Griffith Bolas. He was a journalist and married Elizabeth Grieve Mackenzie in 1908 and they had two children, Cecil Mackenzie Lane and Margaret Lane.

John Lane enlisted in the Royal Sussex Regiment joining it at Chichester on 19th October 1914 as Private John Bolas Lane, service number 4074. He was posted to the 10th (Reserve) battalion, Royal Sussex Regiment on 31st October 1914. His rise in the ranks was meteoric, promoted to Corporal on 1st December 1914 then Sergeant on 1st January 1915. He was subsequently awarded a commission in the 3rd Battalion, Royal Sussex Regiment leaving the 10th Battalion at Sobraon Barracks, Colchester on 21st July 1915 aged 32. His record shows that his military character was 'Very Good' and he was a 'Good Soldier'. His appointment appeared in the Supplement to the London Gazette 21st July 1915 Page 7165.

Having joined the 3rd Battalion, Second Lieutenant Lane attended a training course at the Cambridge University Officer's Training Corps., Cambridge University School of Instruction, Pembroke College, Cambridge, completing the course on 23rd August 1915.

It was about this time that things appear to have started to go wrong for Second Lieutenant Lane. The Commanding Officer of the O.T.C. wrote a report about Second Lieutenant Lane's time on the course reporting that it was not possible to give a certificate to Lane as he did not satisfy the standards of the school in regard to discipline.

> 'On his day as Orderly Sergeant he missed the evening parade and reported later in the Orderly Room in a somewhat unsteady condition. On another occasion he reported present at a lecture-parade but subsequently absented himself from the lecture. His general bearing during the course left much to be desired'
>
> Colonel H.J. Edwards,
> Commanding Officer,
> Cambridge University O.T.C.

On his return to the battalion it appears that the behaviour of Second Lieutenant Lane did not improve. The charge on which he was arraigned in the Court Martial on 10th November 1915 was:

> 'Drunkeness, in that he at Newhaven on 26th October 1915, when in the Ante

> Room, Officer's Mess, 3rd Battalion, Royal Sussex Regiment, at about 9.15 p.m., was drunk'.

In the Court Martial Second Lieutenant Lane was represented by Mr L Tyfield who had been instructed to appear on his behalf by Edells & Cohen, Solicitors of 158, Bishopsgate, London, E.C. On the day following the trial Bells & Cohen wrote to the Judge Advocate General at the War Office submitting that the conviction should be quashed. This was based on the objection to the introduction of the report by the Commanding Officer of the Officer's Training centre which indicated the conduct of the accused on the course and the refusal to allow Second Lieutenant Lane to be recalled to explain the matters referred to in the report. However, no evidence has been found to indicate what action was taken on receipt of the letter.

Second Lieutenant Lane did subsequently pass the course. However, the adjutant of the 3rd Battalion reported that: 'He does not appear to take the slightest interest in his work and 'He has been continually reporting sick and has spent a considerable portion of his service on Sick Leave'. 'I do not consider that he is fitted for the command of men'.

One can only guess at what sort of catastrophic event must have occurred in John Lane's life that had caused such a fine soldier with a very good character to , apparently, become an ill-disciplined officer.

On 14th February 1916 the Commanding Officer of the 3rd Battalion sent a confidential report to the Newhaven Garrison H.Q. with the message:

> 'I am of opinion that the retention in the Service of this officer would not be in the interests of the service'

On 9th March 1916 the Commanding Officer was informed:

> 'in view of the unsatisfactory report on Second Lieutenant (on probation) J.B. Lane, 3rd Battalion, Royal Sussex Regiment, his further retention in the Service cannot be permitted.
>
> He will, therefore, relinquish his commission in the Special Reserve of Officers, and I am to request that he be so informed.
>
> The necessary notification will appear in an early Gazette.'

The notice relinquishing his commission appeared in the Supplement to the *London Gazette* 16th March 1916 Page 2919.

After leaving the army what happened to John Bolas Lane?

Private John Bolas Lane, X/86 of the South African Infantry, 2nd Regiment, served in France and took part in the terrible fighting at Delville Wood during the Battle of the Somme in July 1916. He was killed in action in front of the Butte de Walencourt on 11th October 1916. He is commemorated on the Thiepval memorial, Pier and face 4C.

From, O.C.,
Cambridge University O.T.C.

To, O.C.,
3rd. Battn. Royal Sussex Regt.

Cambridge University School of Instruction.
Pembroke College,
Cambridge.
23. August, 1915.

Sir,

In forwarding to you the reports on the work and conduct of the two Officers of your Battalion who have just completed a Course at this School of Instruction under my Command, I regret to inform you that it was not possible to give a certificate to 2nd. Lieut. J.B.Lane himself, in view of the fact that he did not satisfy the standards of the School in regard to discipline.

On his day of duty as Orderly Sergeant he missed the evening parade, and reported later in the Orderly Room in a somewhat unsteady condition. On another occasion he reported present at a lecture-parade, but subsequently absented himself from the lecture. His general bearing during the course left much to be desired.

I am,
Sir,
Your obedient Servant,
(Sd) H.J.Edwards,
Colonel,
Comdg. Cambridge University O.T.C.

Certified a true copy, [signature]
Capt. & Adjt.,

Training Course Report of 2nd Lieutenant J. B. Lane 23rd August 1915 [NAA]

ON HIS MAJESTY'S SERVICE.

CAMBRIDGE UNIVERSITY.

SCHOOL OF INSTRUCTION.

CERTIFICATE.

Certified that (Temporary) 2nd. Lieutenant LANE J.B. 3rd. Royal Sussex Regt. has attended a class of instruction in the subjects prescribed in War Office letter 43/Miscellaneous/1164 (M.2.3.) of 10 January, 1915.

The report of his work is detailed below:

Elements of drill	Weak
Musketry and Fire Tactics	Very Fair.
Duties of Company Officers in the field	Very Good.
Field Schemes	Poor.
Map reading and use of compas	Poor.
Field entrenchments	Weak.

He has made FAIR progress.

His conduct and discipline have been INDIFFERENT.

(Sd) H.G.Comber,
Major,
Adjutant.

(Sd) R.J.Edwards,
Colonel.

Training Course Certificate of 2nd Lieutenant J. B. Lane [NAA]

EDELLS & COHEN.
SOLICITORS.
S. L. EDELLS
S. COHEN.
Phone 2997 WALL.

9B

158, Bishopsgate,
London, E.C.

26th November 1915.

Sir,

At a General Court Martial held at Newhaven on the 10th and 11th November last, we were instructed to appear in the defence of 2nd Lieutenant, J. B. Lane, of the 3rd Royal Sessex Regiment, who was charged with being drunk in the ante room of the Officers' Mess on the evening of the 26th October, last, at about 9.15 p.mp We instructed Counsel, Mr. L. Tyfield, of 3 Essex Court, Temple, E. C., and who duly appeared as Defendant's counsel.

The trial was opened, and the Court was informed that evidence was to be given on behalf of the accused as to the facts of the case. At the conclusion of the Defendant's case, and after the witnesses to the facts of the case on his behalf had been called, evidence to previous good character was given by Captain St.John Hoskins, who formerly commanded the "A" Company of the 10th Royal Sessex Regiment.

When that evidence had been tendered, the president of the Court asked of the Prosecutor whether he had any evidence in rebuttal as to character. Whereupon the Prosecutor, who was Lieutenant Clayton of the 3rd Royal Sessex Regiment, proceeded to call Captain Nicoll, the adjutant of the accused Officer's Regiment. At that point, Mr. Tyfield, Counsel for the accused, objected to the admissibility of such evidence. It appeared

Solicitors letter to the War Office 26th November 1915 Page 1 of 3 [NAA]

EDELLS & COHEN,
SOLICITORS.
S. L. EDELLS
S. COHEN
Phone 2997 WALL.

(2)

158, Bishopsgate,
London, E.C.

26th November 1915.

to our Counsel that the President of the Court was rather diffident to allow such evidence in rebuttal to character to be introduced before the finding.

The Judge Advocate, however, maintained that it was permissible, and the Court was cleared to consider the objection, but it was eventually decided to admit the evidence. Captain Nicoll thereupon produced to the Court a document purporting to be signed by the Officer commanding the O.T.C. at Cambridge University, and which referred to the accused Officer's conduct. We emphasize the fact that this evidence was given before the finding, and which must have prejudiced the minds of the members of the Court when they came to consider their finding.

We submit that the admission of that evidence in rebuttal to evidence of character before the finding, or at all, was grossly improper and manifestly unfair to the accused Officer. We desire to say further that when an opportunity was asked for the accused Officer to be recalled to explain the matters referred to in the Commanding Officer's O.T.C. of Cambridge University, the Court refused the application.

It was obviously impossible to cross-examine Captain Nicoll in respect of that report.

We submit, therefore the proceedings being irregular, the only course chould be taken in the interests of Justice that

Solicitors letter to the War Office 26th November 1915 Page 2 of 3 [NAA]

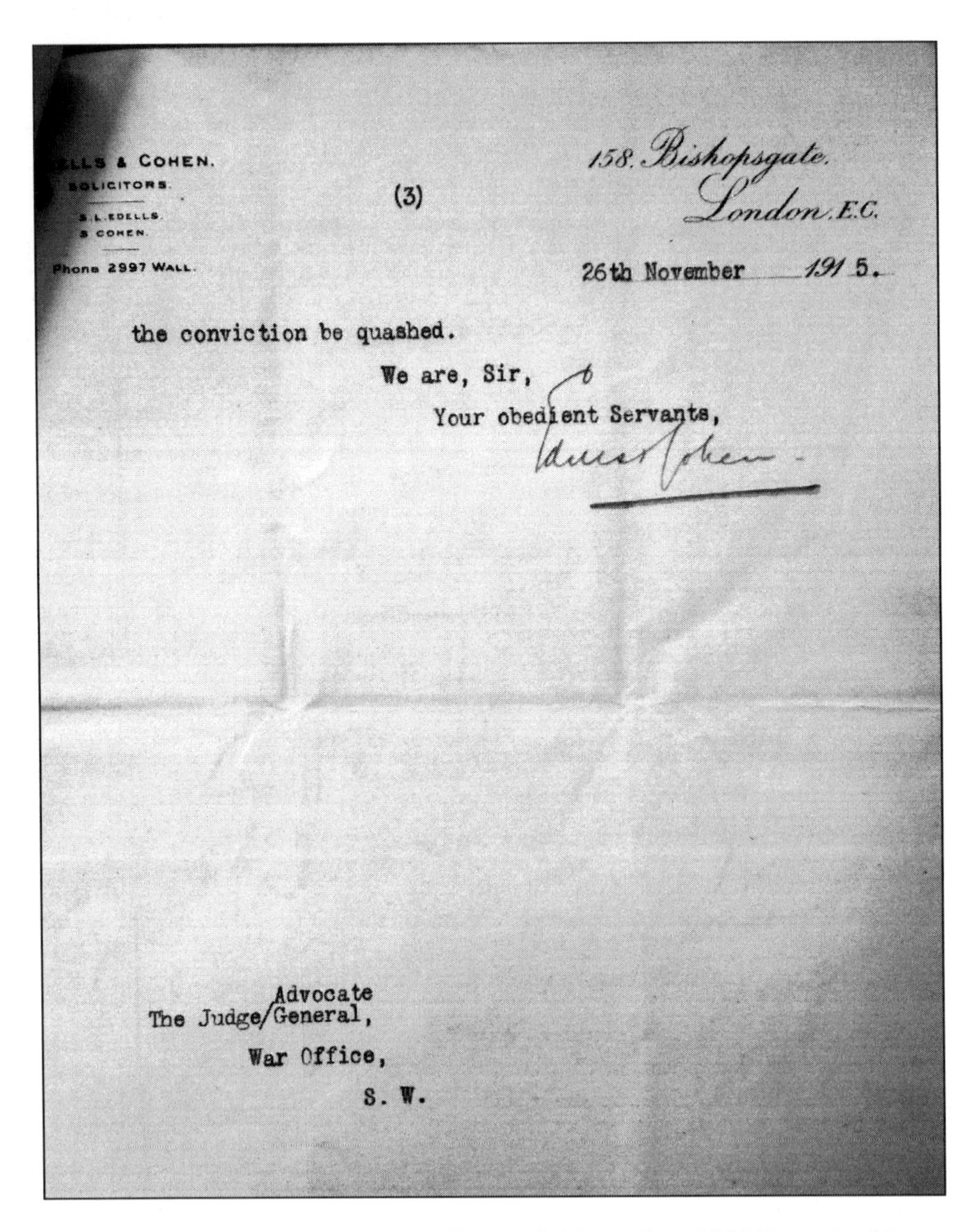

[ED]ELLS & COHEN.
SOLICITORS.
S. L. EDELLS.
S. COHEN.
Phone 2997 WALL.

(3)

158. Bishopsgate.
London. E.C.

26th November 1915.

the conviction be quashed.

We are, Sir,
Your obedient Servants,

Edells & Cohen.

The Judge Advocate General,
War Office,
S. W.

Solicitors letter to the War Office 26th November 1915 Page 3 of 3 [NAA]

BERTRAND RUSSELL AND PRIVATE R.C. ALLEN, 3RD BATTALION, ROYAL SUSSEX REGIMENT

Bertrand Russell (1872-1970) the celebrated philosopher, logician, mathematician, historian and social critic was a prominent anti-war activist. This led to him being banned from certain areas of Britain.

In December 1916 Russell wanted to attend the Court Martial of a friend, Private R.C. Allen to be held in Newhaven. He was denied access to the "Newhaven Special Military Area". However, the then Newhaven Garrison Commander, Lieutenant Colonel C A Hankey issued Russell with a Special Pass. (See copy on following page)

Private R.C. Allen was, in fact, Reginald Clifford Allen, 1st Baron Allen of Hurtwood. He was Secretary and General Manager of the Daily Citizen between 1911 and 1915 and, also, an anti-war activist.

A local newspaper report of 15th December 1916 reported that:-

'A Court Martial, presided over by Major W.A. Dow was held this week on Clifford Allen, chairman of the No-Conscription Fellowship who has only recently been liberated from a sentence of 112 days hard labour at Wormwood Scrubs. The charge was refusing to obey a military order to scour bowls'.

The following week the newspaper for 22nd December 1916 reported that:

> 'RESULT OF LAST WEEKS COURT MARTIAL'
> As a result of the Court Martial held at Newhaven last week Clifford Allen, chairman of the No-Conscription Fellowship, has been sentenced to one year's imprisonment with hard labour for refusing to perform certain duties. With three other conscientious objectors he was taken to Maidstone Prison on Monday.'

Clifford Allen developed tuberculosis of the spine in prison. He was released in December 1917. After the war he was Treasurer and Chairman of the Independent Labour Party between 1922 and 1926, Chairman of the New Leader between 1922 and 1926 and director of the Daily Herald between 1925 and 1930. He married Marjory Gill on 17 December 1921. They had one child. In January 1935 Allen wrote of German dictator Adolf Hitler after he had met him: "I believe Herr Hitler's position in the country is unassailable. His sincerity is tremendous...I am convinced he genuinely desires peace...Germany's aggressive words and warlike phrases do not represent her intentions". Despite his championing of the cause of appeasement, he strongly condemned Nazi brutality and anti-Semitism. His efforts to intercede with the German government trying to save Hans Litten, a prominent opponent of the Nazi regime, from Dachau concentration camp were, however, unsuccessful.

Never having fully recovered from the privations of his imprisonment during the First World War, he died in a sanatorium in Switzerland in 1939, aged 49, when the peerage became extinct.

Permit Book of Bertrand Russell

Page One. Permit Book

Issued at Hunts & Hitch No 90961

Date 1.12.16.

Issued to :—Style or Title Mr

SURNAME (in capitals) RUSSELL

Christian Names Bertrand

Postal Address 57 Gordon Square London W.C.

Signature of Holder Bertrand Russell

PERSONAL DESCRIPTION.

Height 5 ft. 9 ins.

Sex Male

Build Thin

Hair, colour grey

Eyes, colour hazel

Distinctive Marks nil

Entered by

Page Seven Book No 90961

PERMIT No. CANCELLED.

To all whom it may concern.

By virtue of the powers vested in me under the Defence of the Realm Regulations I hereby REFUSE permission to

Mr Bertrand RUSSELL

of 57 Gordon Square London W.C.

to enter

for the purpose of

within the

NEWHAVEN SPECIAL MILITARY AREA

Until

unless withdrawn or otherwise determined.

Special conditions if any Special arrangements will however be made for him to attend the District Court Martial on Pte Allen

Date 6 - DEC 1916 Lieut Colonel Competent Military Authority.

Person(s) in Photograph: Bertrand Russell
Description: This is a page from the Defence of the Realm permit book which was issued to Russell during World War I after his peace activism led to his being banned from certain areas of Britain. Russell had already been convicted and fined for airing his anti-war views, and he served nearly five months of a six month prison sentence handed down in February 1918.
Archive Box Number: RA2 *712
Date: 1916

Description: This is a photograph of another page in Bertrand Russell's permit book. Here he was denied access to the "Newhaven Special Military Area". However, special arrangements were made for him to attend the court martial of his friend Clifford Allen. The Garrison Commander of Newhaven wrote Bertrand Russell the following reply:

"Herewith a Special Pass to enable you to visit Newhaven Special Military Area for the purpose of attending the District Court Martial on Private R.C. Allen. Your Permit Book is also returned. The Pass will not enable you to stay the night in Newhaven, or to go anywhere else in the Town except to the Court Martial room & return to the Station." The letter is dated December 10th, 1916.
Archive Box Number: Russell Archive RA2 *712
Date: 1916

ROYAL ARMY MEDICAL CORPS (R.A.M.C.)

The 1913 War Garrison Accommodation plan showed that it was intended that 3 officers (Civil Practitioners) would be put into private accommodation in Newhaven and 2 Officers & 15 O.R. s accommodated at the Fort. There was a Military Hospital in Newhaven where they worked

In April 1917 the strength of the unit is recorded as being 4 officers and 10 men.

Men known to have served include:-

Major Moulson, Senior M.O. – attended Private A B Saunders who died in hospital on 24th Jan 1917

Captain E.P. Cathcart - attended inquest on Private A B Saunders who died in hospital on 24th Jan 1917

Lieutenant Gilkes – witness at the inquest of Private T Bartram who died 6th Dec 1915. He gave his address as 138 Chapel Street, Newhaven.

Lieutenant Will – witness at the inquest of Private C Clifton who died on 20th April 1916 and Lance Corporal Luft who died 18th April 1916.

Corporal. Frank Johnson - witness at the inquest of Private C Clifton who died on 20th April 1916

Captain R Hill Shaw – attended Sussex RGA Officers Christmas Dinner at the Fort on 25th December 1914.

CAPTAIN B.A. WEST

Captain West was posted to Newhaven in March 1915 where he took up a variety of duties relating to health, hygiene and sanitation. As well as attending daily at the Medical Inspection Room and regularly at Meeching Road Hospital he served as sanitary inspector of the R.G.A. at the Fort and as a member of the Ration Board. He was also responsible for checking the food and hygiene conditions at the Lipton's Establishment where the labourers were fed. In

August Captain West was informed by the War Office that he would shortly be sent on active service. He went on leave at the end of the month and married his fiancée on 1st September. He embarked on active service to Gallipoli landing there on 19th October 1915.

'NEWHAVEN FORTRESS NEWS'

The 'Newhaven Fortress News' was a weekly newspaper produced by the General Recreation Committee composed of officers from the Newhaven Garrison. Copies of issues 5 (20th November 1914) and 10 (24th Dec 1914) obtained from the West Sussex County Archives give the committee members as follows:

Chairman:	Captain P.R. Sanders, Sussex Fortress R.E. (T)
Secretary:	Lieutenant T.H. Vitty, London Electrical Engineers, R.E. (T)
Treasurer:	Lieutenant Duffield Jones , 4th Battalion, Royal Sussex Regiment (T)
Others:	Captain W.H. Grinsted, Sussex R.G.A. (T)
	Second Lieutenant Mayne, Depot, Royal Garrison Artillery

The newspaper contained comments and observations about the war, stories, jokes, poems cartoons etc. and adverts for Newhaven businesses (e.g. Jas. Bannister & Sons, High Street – Outfitters, the Co-operative Society, J.S. Funnell Southdown Bakery, High Street, R. Oxley, Chapel Street – Tobacconist & Newsagent, Harold Grainger, High Street – Chemist, the Electric Theatre, Chapel Street). Details about local churches and their services were included. Readers were encouraged to submit items for inclusion in the paper.

The newspaper was printed and published by the 'Seaford & Newhaven Press, "Chronicle Office", Bridge Street, Newhaven'.

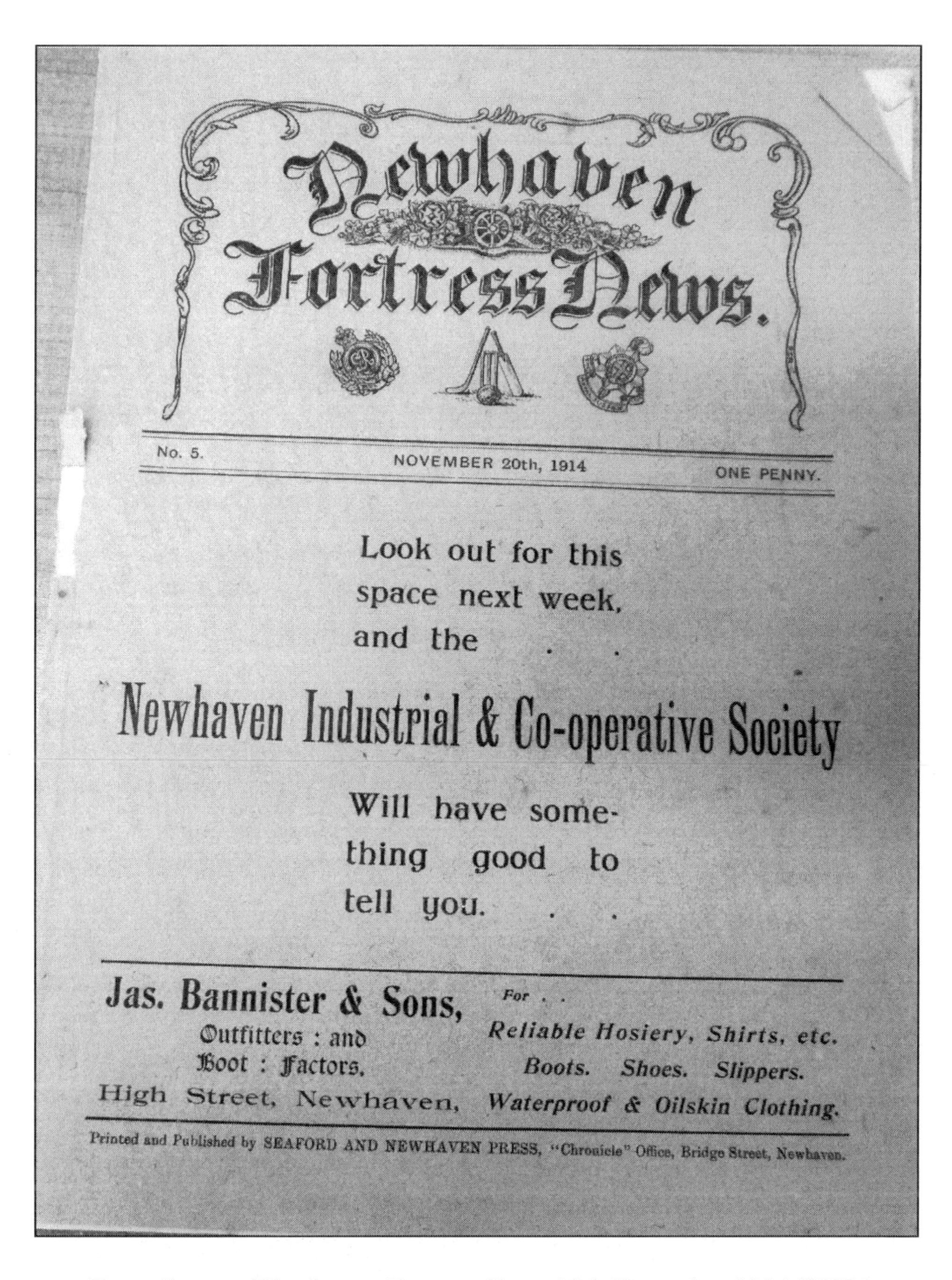

Newhaven Fortress News.

No. 5. NOVEMBER 20th, 1914 ONE PENNY.

Look out for this space next week, and the . .

Newhaven Industrial & Co-operative Society

Will have something good to tell you. . .

Jas. Bannister & Sons,
Outfitters : and Boot : Factors,
High Street, Newhaven,

For . .
Reliable Hosiery, Shirts, etc.
Boots. Shoes. Slippers.
Waterproof & Oilskin Clothing.

Printed and Published by SEAFORD AND NEWHAVEN PRESS, "Chronicle" Office, Bridge Street, Newhaven.

Front Cover of Newhaven Fortress News 20th November 1914 [WSR]

Newhaven Fortress News.

No. 5. November 20th, 1914. Price One Penny.

The Newhaven Fortress News is issued at the instance of the General Recreation Committee, which is composed of the undermentioned Officers:–

Capt. P. R. SANDERS, Sussex Fortress R.E. (T.), *Chairman.*
2nd Lieut. MAYNE, R.G.A. (Depot).
Capt. GRINSTED, Sussex R.G.A. (T.).
Lieut. T. H. VITTY, London Electrical R.E. (T.), *Secretary.*
Lieut. DUFFIELD JONES, 4th Batt. Royal Sussex Regt. (T.), *Treasurer.*

Communications concerning Sports should be addressed to the Secretary, The Fort. Correspondence re Publication should be addressed to the Editor, Sussex Fortress R.E. Camp, Newhaven.

EDITORIAL.

We are introducing a new feature in this week's issue which we hope will meet with universal approval. We refer to the cartoons by "our own Artist."

We hope to be able to give one or two each week. They will for the greater part, be "founded on fact," due licence being given to our lightning Artist, who will be prepared to commemorate and perpetuate any occurrence worthy of that distinction.

So, if any member of this Garrison experiences such an event, and sends us word, the thing shall be done.

Or, if any of you have an especial grudge against a particular chum whom you would like to pillory, send full details along to us and we will allow you to "glut your ire,"—Perhaps!

We find that the Secretarial work occasioned by our increasing circulation (!), is rapidly getting beyond us, and we are therefore asking for additional help.

Don't all speak at once, please, for the appointment is strictly honorary. However, we shall much appreciate the kindly assistance of a gentleman who is sufficiently public-spirited to have a thought for others as well as for himself.

A Syllogism.
The Pen is mightier than the Sword
You all want to be mighty
Therefore, you all want to help us.

Poor Sports! Poor Recreation Ground! What a quagmire!

You'll all have to play "Leap-frog," or "Follow my leader," up and down the cliffs, or start an "Alpine Club" for climbing over the house-tops, if the ground and the weather do not improve.

Weather Retrospect.—"Three white frosts and a —— —— shower."

The article on Engineering this week gives place to an Extract from a pamphlet on "Inoculation."

Those of you who have "suffered" will read it with complacency. But those who have yet that pleasure to come, need not worry about it.

It really doesn't hurt. We *know.*

Our advice is: "Don't think about it—get it over. Above all don't funk. Make light of it; laugh at it; and you'll be surprised at how little it will affect you.

Will all intending contributors please note that *all* articles must be sent, in the first instance, to the Editor, and *not* to the Printer.

Editorial from Newhaven Fortress News 20th November 1914 [WSR]

Extracts from 'The Newhaven Fortress News' of 20th November 1914:

A POEM

The Hours I spend in thee "Oh Fort"
Are as a mouth of bile to me
I count them over every one apart
In Misery. In Misery.

Each hour an oath, each oath a prayer
That I to H.... may be transferred
But day and week and month roll by
My screams remain unheard
Oh Dazzling Beam I watch all night
Oh 6 inch shell of yellow hue
I swear all day and all I get to read
The Fortress News, That rotten Fortress News.

NOTES
(1) These lines do not 'scan'.
(2) The 'abuse' we take as flattery. Our legal friends have a maxim.'If you have no case, abuse your adversary' (Editor)

THINGS WE WANT TO KNOW

1. Who was it who said he had seen a Zeppoplane?
2. What was a certain person doing on the Cliffs to the west of the Fort with a blanket and was he alone?
3. Who is the young officer who talks in his sleep and gives away secrets?
4. Who was it said at Mess the chicken were very high and did he know the chicken were pheasants?
5. Is it true that a certain young officer saw an aeroplane settle on the Fort one dark night?

* * * * *

Cartoon from Newhaven Fortress News [WSR]

TO THE GROUSER

Bread and jam! Bread and jam! Bread and jam again!

Hark the grouser! Hear him complain

It's perfectly true that it's pouring with rain

And the wind whistles by with a shriek like a train.

Cheer up! All the same, you have nothing to gain

By grousing at such like. You might be in pain.

Lying wounded in France or even be slain

By some bloody fat German or girt by a chain

In a deep and dark dungeon that smells like a drain.

It's all for your country. Aren't you too vain

To treat your trials with ought but disdain?

Well! Your duty is clear that with might and with main

You should look on the bright side and never complain.

Everyone's trying with body and brain

To fit you to fight like we did on the Aisne.

And ought but a smile on your honour's a stain,

And the food is not bad and you're awfully well,

There are pleasures in store? You never can tell.

COMPLIMENTARY CONCERT TO THE N.C.O.S OF NO. 1 DEPOT.R.G.A.

An excellent Concert was given at the Sergt's Mess, to the N.C.O.s of the Depot on Thursday evening 12th inst.

Sergt. Roddis was in the chair and was supported by Corpl. Brown ; whilst the "Distinguished Visitors" included Captain Vaux and Lieutenant Brew

There was a very fine array of talent and the programme consisted of many Barrack Room Ballads, interspersed with Toasts and instrumental solos.

Songsters: Sergts. Robinson, Bigwood, Smith and Evans; Brs. Hurst, Gurr, Vickers and Quire; Grs. Couchman and Pearson.
Soloists: Cornet Corpl. Greenhall; Piano Sergt. Parmenter
Toasts: "The Officers of the Depot." In replying Captain Vaux said that he felt uncompetent (sic.) to do so adequately owing to the short period he had been with them, yet he desired, if it should be necessary for him to go to another place, he would choose none other than just across the water. He hoped that if their lot was to go to the front, all of them would go together.

"Our Comrades Abroad." In submitting this toast the Chairman wished it understood that he included not only the men of our own country and the Empire, but the Belgians, French and Russians. Brothers in Arms and companions in Wars and distress; and all those who for us abroad were doing their little bit, which was a much bigger bit than as yet we at home were doing. (Cheers).

"The Junior N.C.O.s." replied to by Br. Batty.

On the conclusion of the programme, and at the suggestion of Lieutenant Brew, the company joined hands and sang "Auld Lang Syne"

The National Anthem concluded the proceedings.

* * * * *

From the "Newhaven Fortress News" dated 24th December 1914:-

CHRISTMAS IN WARTIME

We are now in the midst of Christmas and many of us will find it difficult to realise the fact, as Christmas is always associated with a gathering together of the members of the family, who at this time of the year, more than at any other time, endeavour to spend Christmas at home. For the men at the front this will be impossible and the same holds good for the majority of us here in Newhaven. But at the same time if we are unable to spend Christmas with our families at home owing to the stern necessities of war, let us make up our minds, every one of us, to make it as happy and as joyful a time as possible, remembering that we are all members of one big family fighting for the rights and peace of mankind.

It will be a saddened Christmas time for many with its message of peace where there seems no peace. There is a tendency to dwell too despondently and composedly on the paradox by which, after nearly two thousand years of Christian teaching, millions of men who profess themselves Christians will spend Christmas in at best the merest lull from the greatest war that the world has seen. Yet the note of the soldier's life is not aggression but service and sacrifice; and although such a war as this is an unspeakably horrible calamity, it is not to the same extent a crime. We know that is so when we think of the part in the war that our own relatives and friends are playing or have played out already; and what is true of the share of the individual is also true of the work of them all. It is true also of the great majority of Germans fighting our own sailors and soldiers; for however bad their cause and mistaken their faith in it they make the same sacrifices in its service. Remembering always that sacrifice and service are the essence of the soldier's life, we shall not be so ready to assume that a world-wide war is the most hideous of moral offences, as well as the most fearful of human sufferings. There is probably less cause for moral humiliation in twenty-four hours on the battlefields of Europe than in a single day and night in its cities during time of peace. Atrocities have been committed which will disgrace our age; but they do not preponderate in the lives and deaths and sufferings of so many millions of men. The same holds good of the men who prepared this war, into whose dark minds we do not care to probe for justification; but they, too, must bear their own burdens, and they cannot infect with their responsibility the millions whom they have pitted together in blood.

At home and throughout the British Empire we have peace in spite of it all, and such peace as seldom before. Never in the history of our country has so great a body of its members come forward to vindicate the cause of justice and freedom; and in the common sacrifice and fellowship of all classes the strifes which recently divided us are stilled and recollected, perhaps when we think of them, with shame. In this war many who have been strangers to each other in this nation are learning to know each other; and the nation is truly so homogenous that the stage beyond acquaintance must surely be friendship. Generous words have been spoken by more than one Labour leader in recognition of the promptitude to offer themselves of the rich and high born; and the richer classes have shown a recognition as keen and as just of the great qualities shown by those who have had less training to develop them. Those British people who are impelled by the stress of common experience during this Christmas time to look for points of sympathy rather than of difference in other classes of their countrymen will discover the same national tastes, similar mental standards and the same instinctive loyalties in habit and act. If the poorer can learn that the richer do not always selfishly abuse their advantages, and the richer that ample advantages for the poorer are both due to worth and justified by practical returns, then the inner peace of England and the British Empire in this wartime may endure into the time of peace.

MARS

A regular contributor to the magazine, Mars was "an officer of the Garrison and one of the hardest worked".

From Newhaven Fortress News 24th December 1914 [WSR]

SOLDIER FATALITIES IN NEWHAVEN

It is inevitable that there will be casualties when large groups of men are serving and undergoing training in a military establishment even on home soil, especially during a war situation. The Newhaven Garrison was no exception.

Sadly the men described in the following pages died through accidents or suicide. The details have been obtained from newspaper reports and the records of the inquests that were held at the time.

Private Herbert Charles Jay 10754, 3rd Battalion, Royal Sussex Regiment, 28th May 1915

On 28th May 1915 between 6pm and 7pm, 18 years old Private H.C. Jay was practising alone in the Gymnasium at Newhaven Fort. At the same time Sergeant George Weaver from the same regiment was instructing a class at the other end of the gym.

Sergeant Weaver happened to look across to where Private Jay was practising on the bars just at the moment when Private Jay fell head downwards from the bars onto the mat. Sergeant Weaver rushed to the other end of the gym to render assistance to Jay. The Staff Instructor then took charge of Jay.

Private Jay was taken to St Mark's School Branch of the 2nd Eastern General Hospital in Kemp Town, Brighton where he was diagnosed to be suffering from a fractured spine which caused complete paralysis of his body.

Sadly, Private Jay passed away in the hospital at 4.43 pm on Wednesday 18th August 1915.

At the inquest on 20th August 1915 Lieutenant Colonel Frederick John Paley attached to the R.A.M.C and the 2nd Eastern General Hospital gave evidence that Private Jay died from 'Exhaustion the result of the paralysis'.

Sergeant Weaver explained that Private Jay was attempting to do what is known as 'the back lift' when he fell from the bars.

The verdict was 'Accidental Death'.

Private Jay was the son of George Mathias Jay an architect and surveyor of 36 St. Aubyns Road, Portslade.

Private Thomas Bartram, GSSR/67, No. 8 Company, 3rd Battalion, Royal Sussex Regiment, 6th Dec 1915

Private Bartram was found dying from a rifle shot in the Musketry Storeroom at Newhaven Fort at 10.45 a.m. on 6th December 1915. He had committed suicide yet his death could and should have been avoided.

Thomas Bartram was born in Glastonbury, Somerset in 1864 and had served in the army prior to the outbreak of the Great War. He was aged 51when he died. He was 19 when he attested as a Gunner with the Royal Artillery in May 1884, joining the R.A. at Fort Rowner, Gosport on 1st June 1884 and his service number was 49244. He had been a railway porter in civilian life.

Gunner Bartram went to Egypt arriving there 30th August 1884 and serving there until 2nd November 1885. He was awarded the Egypt Medal with clasp for the Nile 1884-85.

During his time in Egypt the climate did not suit him. Gunner Bartram was hospitalised for 6 days with Conjunctivitis, 17 days with Dysentery, 68 days with Enteric Fever and, on 25th September 1885, was diagnosed with "General Disability". He was sent back to England where he spent a further 23 days in hospital at Woolwich. After recovering he was posted to 3/1 Southern Div. However, he was again hospitalised with Debility on 15th February 1886 and after appearing at a medical board at Dover on 7th June 1886 he was declared unfit for further service due to "Debility" and discharged from the service on 25th June 1886.

His Royal Artillery service papers carried the following note:

> 'Found to have improperly enlisted into 2nd Battalion, Royal Sussex Regiment as no. 2905 Private Edwin Barton – Trial dispensed with under Sec. 161 Army Act. Held to serve on last attestation. Dr 19330.'

This note was a cross-reference to the service papers for Private Edwin Barton 2905, 2nd Battalion, Royal Sussex Regiment for service from 21st August 1888 to 30th March 1897. This was Thomas Bartram who had enlisted under an assumed name. He had attested at Aldershot on 21st August 1888 and claimed he was born in Freemantle, Southampton and had not previously served in the services. However, in both his R.A. service papers and his Royal Sussex Regiment service papers he gave his next of kin as Mrs Taylor, East Creetch, Wareham, Dorset.

Thomas had served under the name of Edwin Barton initially in the 1st Royal Sussex and then the 2nd Royal Sussex in the U.K. from 21st August 1888 to 31st December 1889 and then in India with the 2nd Royal Sussex from 1st January 1890 to 30th March 1897 when he was invalided back home to the U.K. He was declared medically unfit for service and discharged. Whilst no details of his health during his service are known his service papers are endorsed with the word "Insane". The date this endorsement was made is unknown.

When war broke out Thomas Bartram again enlisted in the army attesting at Chichester on 20th August 1914 as a Private with the Royal Sussex Regiment. He did mention his previous 12 years service with the regiment. Thomas went to France on 23rd November 1914 where he served in the trenches. He was admitted to hospital in Rouen with bronchitis on 31st January 1915 but returned to the U.K. on 9th Feb 1915. He subsequently arrived in Newhaven from Dover on 16th May 1915.

At this time Thomas's sister, Mary Taylor, was extremely concerned about the mental state of her brother. On 23rd September 1915 she wrote to the C.O. of the Royal Sussex Regiment from her home in East Creech near Wareham:

> 'Sir,
> I am writing to you on behalf of my brother, Private T Bartram, No. 67, 9th Com 3rd Batt. Asking you if you will see to him on his behalf as he is suffering Mentally. He has been twice invalided out of the Army with same complaint. When the war broke out last year he joined up again & served 3 months in the trenches. His proper age is 53 but he put it back to 45 as he badly wanted to do his part for his country & I should be very sorry to see him go wrong again as I am the only one he has to look to.
>
> I have got his last discharge papers from Netley Hospital with a good character. Trusting you will help me as I am ill myself & cant stand so much worry. I have enclosed the last letters I had from him.'

The letters that Thomas wrote to his sister showed his mental state (a few words are illegible or missing from the images of the letters) *illegible day/month 1915*

'Dear Sister,

I am foolish to keep you waiting for a letter as I know you must feel anxious about me. I thank you and Nellie very much for trying to speak on my behalf but I am afraid it wont do any good. I would not mind a fig if I felt all-right as what I am doing now is childs play as compared to the trenches last winter.

I know what's the matter it's low spirits mental depression whitch you know is worse than bodyily illness. The men in the Hut know there is something wrong but then you know you cant tell strangers your feelings. I am ashamed to think that I cant buck up But I pray God that it will weare off soon its a bad feeling to say the least of it and I did so want to pull through and at the end of the war come down and help old Charlie a bit and now if I can only have a change and you to talk to I am sure things would brighten for me I cant seem to rally at all hear. I have nothing to complain of and my Sergent Major Bill Fleet have shown every consideration for me. You need not alarm yourself I mean to hold on to the last hopeing against hope that I shall feel better soon if I only had the heart I could get a privilidge ticket .... London and come down for a few days But then you see I would not be able to resist stopping with you and of course that would not do I haven't got into any trouble yet but I can see it coming if I cant pull myself together soon.

You can let Mrs Fox [?] know how I am and say I should have written but no heart to do so Love also to little Jim and all of them.

Now dear sister I will say good night and love to you and old Charlie and Nellie and Aggie hoping poor dear Plowie is getting better as she is only just starting out in life. We have had some nice weather and I hope Charlie as got up is potatoes in .... condition drop a line ....and say what you th(ink?)....It might be but I cant do it I am really too old to stand the... I cant get any sleep I want and... Tom.'

and

13 1915

My Dear Sister I am very sorry indeed to keep you in anxiety for a letter from me But to tell you the truth I cant help it I am so much run down and feel so nervous and bad that I haven't the heart to do anything. I am suffering agony

> in my head I cant get any sleep its no use telling our doctors. You know Polly I ought not to have joined up its just as I was when I came home from India and I don't think I can stick it much longer. If the war office [knew] I was invalided out with the same thing Mentally wrecked they might send me out my regimental number was 2905 Ed Barton. You might get someone to try what can be done for God sake do if you can as I [am] awfull bad. I shant say anymore as I don't want to upset you Your loving
>
> Brother Tom
>
> Love to poor old Charlie and all of you
>
> I got the tobbacco all right

Mary Taylor did get a response from the adjutant of the Royal Sussex regiment and she wrote to him on 6th October 1915.

> Sir,
>
> I now write and thank you for your letter on behalf of my brother Pte T Bartram & very glad to hear you are going to do something for him. I have enclosed his last letter in which he said he as not heard anything about this so I trust you will soon do something for him as his letters are such a worry to me & I am not very strong that I cannot stand the worry of it, but I should feel very sorry if he was to cause any further trouble.
>
> I am yours Obedient
>
> Mary Taylor

Despite Mary Taylors letter to the regiment and the assurance given her it appears that little, if anything, was done. The inquest proceedings into the circumstances of Thomas's death were reported in the local newspaper.

> 'Lieutenant Gilkes of 138 Chapel Street, Newhaven the M.O. said that the death was caused by a rifle shot. Lieutenant Clayton stated that the deceased was an old soldier. He had served in the Army for 12 years, part of the time in India. He re-enlisted in London on 20th August 1914. He was a single man and was within a few days of his 42nd birthday when he re-joined. He was passed by the doctor as being fit for the Army Reserve. His conduct had been satisfactory. He was punished on the Saturday preceding his death by Lieutenant Clayton as

his Company officer, for a minor offence in the lines, the punishment being 7 days confined to barracks. It was the usual punishment for this class of offence.

Private Bartram came to the Fort from Dover on 16th May 1915 and was attached to No. 8 Company, 3rd Royal Sussex Regiment and had been employed as Musketry Store Keeper for the last six weeks and appeared to be alright. But on the morning of Monday 6th December at 10.45 a.m. he shot himself.

Sergeant Thomas Elliott of 'C' Company, Royal Sussex Regiment, who was working in the Tailor Shop which is separated by a 7 ft high match-boarding partition from the Musketry Store when he heard what sounded like a crack from a rifle and a heavy thud and on looking over the partition saw Private Bartram lying on his back with a miniature rifle lying across his legs and blood coming from his mouth. Sgt Elliott said to his mates 'He's shot himself!' He at once went to fetch a Military Doctor who ordered his removal to the Military Hospital but he had died before they removed him.

Lieutenant Gilkes, R.A.M.C. said that he was called to see the deceased shortly after 10 o'clock on Monday morning. He was bleeding from the head from what was apparently a miniature rifle bullet wound in the inner corner of the right eye. The bullet went out at the back of the head. He was unconscious and stopped breathing but his pulse was still beating. This stopped about half a minute after Lieutenant Gilkes had arrived. From the direction of the wound it was almost impossible to be other than self-inflicted. From the evidence he would say that the deceased was suffering from nervous depression. He was apparently run down and on his papers he was reported to be suffering from debility.

Sergeant John Naldrett of No.5 Company, 3rd Royal Sussex Regiment said that Private Bartram came to the musketry office at 10 minutes to nine on the previous Monday morning and he was there at 10.40 when Sergeant Naldrett went to the coffee shop. Private Bartram was cleaning the miniature rifles which was part of his daily duty. He was a quiet man and used to mumble at his work. At first Sergeant Naldrett used to answer him but latterly he did not take any notice of this, as he had his clerical work to do. He had been working with Private Bartram for two or three months.

Mr A Akhurst, a juror, asked if it was possible for a cartridge to have been left in one of the miniature rifles and for this to be fired accidentally.

Sergeant Naldrett replied that this was impossible as the rifles were always cleaned on the range before being returned to store and he always pulled the bolts to the full extent so it was impossible for a cartridge to be left in.

The coroner stated that a strict check was kept on the issue and use of ammunition Private Bartram went on to the miniature rifle range when firing was in progress and it was his duty to stick the cartridges into a band ready for the man who was firing. Thus he might have been able to get possession of a cartridge or two. Sergeant Naldrett said that when he returned to the musketry store he found the deceased lying on the ground with a miniature rifle across him, the butt being under his right leg and the barrel across his left leg Two other soldiers were present and he removed the rifle (which was produced together with the deceased's cap which had a small hole through the crown.)

Private Ernest Beckett of the Royal Sussex Regiment said he slept in the same hut as Private Bartram. On Tuesday of the previous week, Private Beckett had suggested a game of cards in the evening. He thought Private Bartram looked bad and said to him 'What's the matter old chap? You're looking rather queer'. Bartram replied 'I'm getting sick of this being ordered about so much. I shall throw myself over the cliffs or shoot myself'. He did not say anything further but went to bed earlier than usual that evening. Private Beckett did not think Bartram meant what he said seriously.

Corporal Bartlett said that he was not in the deceased's Company but last Saturday evening he was sitting with him in front of the fire. Private Bartram was looking very down-hearted about something and asked him what was the matter. Private Bartram said he did not know but he was 'fed up with everything' and he said it was through getting into trouble over nothing at all. No doubt he was referring to the punishment he had received. On Sunday Bartram was very quiet and strange and went to bed in the afternoon which was unusual for him. On Monday morning shortly after 8 o'clock, Corporal. Bartlett was tidying up the hut when Private Bartram remarked 'Corporal, I shall put my kit in my bag, as I shan't want it anymore'. Corporal. Bartlett did not know what he meant. He thought perhaps he had orders to move from his quarters as he was liable to be shifted at any time. Corporal. Bartlett had not the slightest suspicion that he referred to committing suicide.

Lance Corporal. Albert Watson of No. 8 Company, 3rd Royal Sussex Regiment said he had known Private Bartram since November 13th. He had never heard him complain of his treatment until last Friday. Private Bartram was absent from the Pay Parade on that day, probably owing to his duties and in the evening he went to his Company Office. He looked rather strange and Lance Corporal Watson remarked that he looked bad. Private Bartram said he felt bad and 'was fed up'. He seemed depressed and made the remark that if those at the top only knew the ills of some of the men perhaps they would not be so funny. Lance Corporal. Watson supposed that he referred to someone at the top camp with reference to his punishment.

In reply to the Jury Foreman Lieutenant Clayton said Private Bartram's punishment of 7 days c.b. extended from last Saturday to next Saturday. He had not been punished before. Lieutenant Clayton did not think the punishment was severe. Pte, Bartram had complained of feeling unwell and had written to his sister complaining about his head but had not reported himself sick. The punishment 'confined to barracks' meant that a man was not allowed to leave the camp and he had to answer every roll call. A man had also had certain fatigue duties to perform, but Private Bartram being on special duty would not have to perform fatigues. When asked if it was possible for a man to get more than 7 days for this offence, Lieutenant Clayton replied only if he had been sent to the Commanding Officer when he could get 10 days c.b.

Lieutenant Gilkes, R.A.M.C. confirmed that the Company Officer would not be aware of Private Bartram's condition as he had not reported that he was sick. No officer knowing that a man was sick would punish him. In this case the punishment was actually a kindness in disguise because it meant that Private Bartram would get rest from going out in the town which, owing to his age and state of health, was what he really needed.

The Foreman asked 'He evidently did not consider it a kindness in disguise?' Lieutenant Gilkes replied 'No'.

Mr Gay, a Juror, remarked that the punishment would no doubt increase Private Bartram's feeling of depression. For debility a man would not necessarily be put on the sick list in the present circumstances.

The Coroner, in summing up, said he did not think he was in a position to say whether the punishment was excessive or not in this case. On the face of it the punishment was not severe and the offence may not have been very serious in itself, though laymen did not know how these matters were regarded in the Army. He thought they must accept it as a fact that it was a punishment allowed by the military regulations, and that the Company Officer was competent to

> impose such a punishment. Private Bartram's abnormal state of mind was not known by his officer, and the punishment would no doubt affect a man in that state of mind more than if he was in a normal state of health bodily and mentally. The Company Officer or anybody else had no reason to suppose that imposing a sentence of 7 days confinement to barracks would cause a man to commit suicide. It would be unreasonable to suppose that a set back or repression of this sort imposed by a superior in the discharge of duty would lead a man to act in that way. If the Jury did think the punishment was excessive, of course, they could add a rider to their verdict, though what the effect of that would be he could not say. The question for the Jury appeared to be one of fact – whether Private Bartram intended to take his life or not.
>
> The Jury, after a short retirement, returned a verdict of 'Suicide during temporary insanity'.

The statement from the inquest that *"Private Bartram's abnormal state of mind was not known by his officer"* is damning. It is apparent that the officer in charge did not follow through and read the contents of Thomas's letters and investigate Thomas's service records as requested by his sister or, if he did, there was a failure in communication to Thomas's immediate superior. At the very least Thomas should have been discharged from service.

The inevitable conclusion is that the punishment of 7 days Confined to Barracks tipped poor Thomas over the edge.

Private Bartram was buried in Newhaven Cemetery. His sister acknowledged her receipt of his 1914/15 Star, Victory and British War medals on 9th September 1919.

Name.	Corps.	Rank.	Regtl. No.
BARTRAM Thomas.	R. SUSS R	Pte	GSSR/64
	-"-	-"-	-"-

Medal.	Roll.	Page.	Remarks.
VICTORY	E/2/101 B21.	4669	D of W 6-12-15
BRITISH	-do-	-do-	
15 STAR	E/2/2/B1	26	

Theatre of War first served in	(1) France
Date of entry therein	23-11-14

K 1380.

Medal Index Card for Private Thomas Bartram [NAA]

Headstone of Private Thomas Bartram in Newhaven Cemetery 2013 [NFA]

Lance Corporal Elias Luff, L/4705, 3rd Battalion, Royal Sussex Regiment, attached to Newhaven Garrison Military Police 18th April 1916

Elias Luff was the son of Mrs Susan Luff, and was a native of Fulking. He had enlisted in Brighton in 1894 when he was a labourer. He had served 22 years in the army and spent part of that time in India with the Royal Sussex regiment. He went to France on 12th August 1914 with the 2nd Battalion, Royal Sussex Regiment at the outbreak of the war and was wounded in 1915. He suffered shrapnel wound to his right hand index finger and a thorn also penetrated the same finger. The finger turned septic causing him to be invalided home and on 9th June 1915 the finger was amputated at the 2nd Eastern General Hospital. Afterwards he went on sick leave for a time then was posted to 3rd Battalion, Royal Sussex Regiment at Newhaven where he was attached to the Newhaven Garrison Military Police. He was now 41 years of age and was about two months from securing his discharge from the army as a time-expired man.

On 14th April 1916 Sergeant Harry Barnard of the Garrison Military Police noticed that Lance Corporal Luff was looking unwell and said he thought he had a touch of the fever that he contracted in India. Sergeant Barnard told him to 'go sick' and report to the hospital. He was a little light-headed but talked sensibly. Lance Corporal Luff was admitted to the Newhaven Military Hospital and paraded before the Colonel who instructed that he be sent to bed.

Lieutenant Will, R.A.M.C., stated that Lance Corporal Luff was suffering a feverish attack probably caused by influenza. The influenza was of a mild character but it very often led to depression

On Sunday 16th April he was discovered attempting to cut his throat in bed and before he was stopped he had succeeded in severing his windpipe to a large extent. The wound in the throat was stitched up but on Tuesday 18th April Lance Corporal Luff had a relapse and his temperature rose to 106 and he subsequently died.

Lieutenant Will, R.A.M.C., testified that a good deal of pneumonia followed the injury and was caused by air reaching the lungs through the wound not purified as it would be by passing through the nose. Death resulted from septic pneumonia resulting from the wound in the throat.

A verdict of 'Suicide during temporary insanity bought on by influenza' was returned.

Elias was buried in Portslade cemetery.

Elias was awarded the 1914 Star with Clasp, the British War Medal and Victory Medal. His Medal Index Card states that he died of wounds 18th April 1916.

35

Name.	Corps.	Rank.	Regtl. No.
LUFF Elias	2/R Suss R	Pte	L/4705

Medal.	Roll.	Page.	Remarks.
VICTORY	E/2/101 B22	4712	D of W 18/4/16
BRITISH	do	do	Returned (1743 K.R.) 7860/Add
14 STAR	E/2/2	66	
Clasp/2/2689			1914 Star Clasp Retd for disposal CRV oy. 26.2.25 NW/9/4106 217/B
Theatre of War first served in			
Date of entry therein	12-8-14		NW/9/4106. 7860/Add K 1380.

Medal Index Card for Private Elias Luff [NAA]

Private Cecil Clifton, 5124, 3rd Battalion, Royal Sussex Regiment, 20th April 1916

Private Cecil Clifton was off-duty at the time when he met his death while cycling downhill in Newhaven on Thursday 20th April 1916.

Private Clifton was aged 20, married and his wife, Gwendoline Irene Clifton lived at 2, Sea View, Chapel Street, Newhaven. Prior to enlisting in February 1916 he was a druggist's porter.

Corporal Arthur Soal, 3rd Royal Sussex, stated that he did not know Private Clifton personally but on Thursday, between the Hospital and South Road while walking downhill on the pavement, he saw Private Clifton pass him on a bicycle. Private Clifton was shouting as he went down saying he had lost control of the bicycle and did not know how to stop. He was going down the hill at great speed and in trying to turn right he failed to do so and 'dashed' into a wall.

Corporal Frank Johnson, R.A.M.C. stated that while in South Road at 5.00 pm on the Thursday he heard a crash. He went to where Private Clifton lay unconscious and found he had been dashed against a wall and window, which was broken. Corporal Johnson sent for assistance and had Private Clifton removed to hospital.

Private Frederick Maidlow stated that Private Clifton was a friend of his, that he owned the bicycle and had loaned it to Private Clifton at 3.15 pm that day. Private Maidlow had told Private Clifton that the bike was not fit to ride as the brake was damaged. However, Private Clifton said that he would fix it. It transpired that Private Clifton had tried to fix the bike but had failed to do so. He wanted the bike for a pleasure ride and not for duty or business.

Private Clifton was familiar with the town and his widow testified that he had been used to riding a bicycle.

Lieutenant Will, R.A.M.C, explained that Private Clifton had fractured the base of his skull. When taken to hospital Private Clifton was unconscious and did not recover his senses.

The jury returned a verdict that Private Clifton had met his death accidentally. The Coroner remarked that "it was a matter of regret that another useful man should be lost to his country at this time".

Lance Corporal Arthur Thomas Twine, G/5639, 3rd Battalion, Royal Sussex Regiment, 16th Jan 1917

Lance Corporal Arthur Thomas Twine (G/5639) of the 3rd Battalion of the Royal Sussex Regiment (RSR) died on 16th January 1917 aged 19. He is buried at the Havant and Waterloo (Warblington) Cemetery.

He lived at 3 The Gardens, Emsworth, Hampshire with his mother Mrs Elizabeth J Twine. His father was dead and he had an older brother Eddie George Twine. His brother last saw him on 3rd January 1917 when he was home on leave. Before the war, Arthur was a gardener.

Although only 19 years of age, Lance Corporal Twine had been in the army nearly two years, having enlisted in April 1915, and had already been to the Front and been wounded twice.

Lance Corporal Twine accidently lost his life while drilling on the downs about one mile west of Newhaven. Lieutenant Frederick Y Goring, of the RSR, took the training company onto the Downs to the West of Newhaven on Tuesday morning. They arrived about 9:30 am and were split into four parts, each under a sergeant. Lance Corporal Twine was under Company Sergeant Major (CSM) Peacham. There were 25 men in this platoon and each platoon sergeant would choose his own ground to drill on.

The distance, from where the platoon stood in close formation to the cliff edge, was 78 paces (this was paced out following the accident). The cliff, at this point, was a shear drop of 100 feet. The order was given by CSM Peacham "To the right, three paces extend". This meant that each man would double out in single file three paces apart. In carrying out this order, the men would move to the right with their heads turned over their left shoulder, in order to judge the correct distance between each man. Each man would therefore be looking away from the cliff edge. The sergeant major would be facing the men. Lance Corporal Twine was on the extreme right of the row, closest to the cliff edge.

When asked, Lieutenant Goring confirmed that they were not limited for space and there was no need for them to be so close to the cliff edge. CSM Peacham was an experienced man, and although Lieutenant Goring didn't know how much service he had he said he was "a man who knew his job". They had been drilling at that spot about half a dozen times before and the whole battalion would sometimes go out there, but then probably only drill in close formation rather than extended order. As far as Lieutenant Goring was aware there hadn't been any accidents in the past.

Private Charles George Dean was in the same platoon as Twine and in the rank (row) behind him, also at the far right. He described how LC Twine was running along looking over his left shoulder. The Coroner asked him if this was the correct thing to do, to which he replied "Yes, Sir" and confirmed that they were all running "as fast as we could go". Luckily for Private Dean, he looked round just before he reached the edge, stopping one foot away from it and in time to see Lance Corporal Twine fall. Private Dean then got down on his hands and knees and looked over the edge and saw Lance Corporal Twine falling. He ran back before Twine had reached the bottom and reported the incident. Private Dean was asked if they realised they were so close to the cliff edge. He explained that he thought it was just a gradual slope down the other side, like the one they had just come up.

Lance Corporal Barrett reported the accident to CSM Peacham, who ran over to the spot where Lance Corporal Twine had fallen. Private Dean didn't hear CSM Peacham say anything. Lieutenant Goring was instructing one of the platoons when he saw CSM Peacham running towards him. He reported that Lance Corporal Twine had fallen over the cliff.

CSM James Arthur Peacham was then called to give evidence. He explained that shortly after the order was given to extend, someone had shouted that a man had fallen over the cliff. He immediately ran over to the spot where the man had fallen and then reported it to Lieutenant Goring. No one had come and reported the incident to him. Following the accident, CSM Peacham stepped the distance from where Lance Corporal Twine had been standing and found it to be 78 paces to the cliff edge. There were 13 men in the front rank (row) which meant there were 91 paces for the men to extend into, leaving 16 paces from the extreme right hand man (i.e. Lance Corporal Twine) and the cliff edge. The only reason he could give for Lance Corporal Twine going over the edge was the men's keenness in doing the work, by which he meant that some may have gone further than their 3 paces. "One man might go a little more than three paces and some a little less, but it would come very nearly right in the end." He explained that he wasn't familiar with the ground and wasn't aware that they were so close to the cliff edge, although he believed that the men had done the same movement there before, as they were already in close formation when he took over.

Lance Corporal Robert Barrett, giving evidence after CSM Peacham, explained that he was the third from Lance Corporal Twine in the single rank. He had just doubled out when he turned to the front and saw Lance Corporal Twine step over the edge of the cliff, hearing him cry out "Oh!" as he went over. Lance Corporal Barrett had no idea they were so close to the cliff edge. He called out that a man had fallen over the cliff and the sergeant-major had replied "Go down and fetch him". Afterwards, CSM Peacham said he couldn't remember making the remark, but explained that, at the time, he hadn't realised how serious the accident was. He believed Lance Corporal Twine might have tripped over an obstacle like a gorse bush, as sometimes happened during this type of movement.

The jury concluded that it was a case of "Accidental Death", but expressed the opinion that the Military Authorities should ensure that instructors survey the ground before drilling their men there.

Lance Corporal Arthur Twine's body was transported from the Military Hospital to the Railway Station, by gun carriage, at mid-day Friday for burial at his home town of Emsworth. The procession was led by the Battalion Band and included officers, non-commissioned officers and the men from Lance Corporal Twine's company. As the coffin was placed in a special railway van, the buglers sounded The Last Post.

Private Allen Bernard Sanders, 19561, 3rd Battalion, Royal Sussex Regiment, 24th Jan 1917

Private Sanders, aged 22, died in the Military Hospital, Newhaven during the evening of Wednesday Jan 24th 1917. He had undergone Gas Training during the afternoon of that day and had experienced difficulties during the training which caused him to exit the gas chamber prematurely. Although he initially confirmed that he was feeling better his condition worsened and he was taken to hospital where it was confirmed that he had been gassed. He died shortly afterwards.

Private Sanders had only been in the army for a few months and before joining up he was articled to a surveyor. Julia Sanders of 61, Carlisle Road, Hove , who was very deaf, identified the body as that of her son.

Staff Captain Montgomery RGA supplied details of Private Sander's attestation and calling up dates and also his medical history and conduct which had been satisfactory.

Captain P Price, Royal Field Artillery, Newhaven Area Anti-Gas School provided a statement of the circumstances leading to the demise of Private Sanders (with the incorrect spelling of his name!), (see pages 143 and 144).

Details of the inquest appeared in the local press:

Private Ernest Plews, Royal Sussex Regiment, one of the men who went in with Private Sanders said Sanders seemed to him to be hysterical, throwing his arms and legs about and, at first, he thought he was playing the fool. Plews thought him a very nervous man and as Sanders crossed the room he put his hands at the back of his head and tried to take his equipment off. Plews pulled Sander's arms down and kept them down and led him out. He went willingly, but staggered.

Dr. Hugh Miller Galt, pathologist to the Royal Sussex County Hospital, gave

Re. Private A. B.Saunders.3rd. Royal Sussex Regiment.

Brief statement of the circumstances by Capt. P. Price.RFA.Newhaven Area Anti-Gas School.

On Wednesday afternoon January 24th, 1917, at about 3-30 I had a party of men belonging to the 3rd.Royal Sussex Regiment to pass through the gas chamber, the number being One hundred and sixteen (116). Before each man leaves the parade ground, which is in the vicinity of the chamber, he is inspected in order, to see that his Gas Helmet is efficiently tucked away underneath the Tunic, also that he has it properly adjusted upon his head, this was carried out by Lance-Corporal Parker and Private Worsell of my Staff, they were also upon this particular day seen by an NC.O.of the 3rd. Royal Sussex Regt.named Sergt.Avis.

The men are then marched off to enter the chamber in batches of 25.

The first two batches of men were passed through the chamber quite successfully, but prior to entering the chamber in each instance I halted the men just outside, to instruct them that, under no circumstances whatever was any man to interfere with his helmet inside the chamber, and not until he had passed through the gas and paraded again on the ground just above the chamber.

They were next asked if every man was breathing alright in his helmet, to which they all replied "Yes".I then cautioned them that if any man felt a bit nervous whilst in the chamber, he must put up his hand, when he would be immediately let out. After this had been done, I gave instructions for the men to be taken inside the chamber, with Lieut. Feasey and Corporal Matthews.

Then when ~~they~~ two batches were released another batch of 25 men came along to go through among which was the deceased(Private Saunders).before entering the chamber this batch was cautioned in the same way as the previous ones, and no complaints of any description were made by any of the men. I gave instructions for them to be taken in the chamber.The door was closed and after about five seconds had elapsed, it was opened, and out came two men, I called to them not to touch their helmets, and to come to me, which they did.They were asked by me to remove their helmets. I then asked them their reason for coming out of the chamber, to which they replied that they could not breathe properly in the helmet. I told them to go on to the parade ground. About two or three seconds after I saw the door of the gas chamber open, and the Corporal put a man outside at the same time telling him not to touch his helmet, but to go to the top. I also called to him not totouch his helmet, and to come to me, but he did not seem to hear me, and when went a step or two the other way.

Statement of Captain P. Price R.F.A. [ESR]

(2).

immediately dashed forward to him, and with the assistance of Private Plews walked him over to the bank of earth near the hut. I took off his helmet, and threw it upon the ground, after which I laid the deceased down, at the same time telling him not to get excited. I next administered to him a phial of ammonia upon a handkerchief to inhale through his mouth, after a few minutes I asked him if he was feeling better to which he replied" I feel much better now Sir" I then called to Lieut. Feasey to examine his helmet very carefully, and after doing so he pronounced it quite sound. I then asked the deceased if he felt or tasted anything inside the Gas chamber, ad he replied "No". After this I showed the deceased the helmet he had worn, in order that he might see that it was quite safe, and he was satisfied with it. I then asked him if he was nervous and he replied"Yes" I next asked him if he had a cold and he replied"Yes" that he had, had one all week upon his chest. After resting him for a while, I assisted him around the back of the Gas chamber to the parade ground at the top of the cliff, and told him to get a little fresh air, when he had been there for about five minutes I had him assisted down to camp, upon the way I asked him several times if he was feeling better, and he replied each time "Yes". Half way to the camp I stopped and had adminetered to him another phial of ammonia, as he seemed to be in a state of exhaustion, this administration seemed to relieve him, so the journey was continued to the camp were he was placed in a motor car and conveyed to the Military Hospital, and seen there by Major Moulson, the Senior Medical Officer, who ordered him to be put to bed at once. I then asked Major Moulson to examine him, and let me know the result which he did, and gave it as his opinion that the man had been gassed. I then reported the case by telephone to the Chemical Adviser Eastern Command.

P. Price

Capt.

Newhaven Area Anti-Gas School.

Statement of Captain P. Price R.F.A. [ESR]

the results of the post mortem that he had made. He found the lungs and the chest waterlogged like those of a drowned man. The condition of the lungs was such that had the deceased been a normal individual the experience should not have killed him. The stomach contents indicated that he had bolted his food in a nervous state and his stomach had refused to act. The cause of death was asphyxia from the condition of the lungs. To an average individual the experience would have been quite unimportant. He had no doubt that when he went into the apartment the deceased held his breath as long as possible – the worse thing he could do.

Answering a question by the foreman of the jury Captain E.P. Cathcart M.D. said that morning he himself went into the apartment and stood a test five times stronger and for three or four times the length of time the deceased did without any effect. The equipment should be good for six hours continuous use, but for the most part men were subjected to the test for from two to four minutes and rarely longer than five minutes.

The verdict of the inquest was 'Death by Misadventure'. The jury considered that death was due to asphyxia while undergoing training at a time when Private Sanders was in a highly nervous condition being also of an abnormally nervous constitution. No blame was attached to any of the officers or men concerned in the training and also that the appliances in use were not at fault.

Private Sanders was buried in Hove Old Cemetery.

NEWHAVEN PORT STATISTICS

Between 14th August 1914 and 11th November 1918 Newhaven Port employed some 2700 civilian labourers at different times and processed the following:

Troops Embarked	Officers	104
	Men	9,504
	TOTAL	9,608
Returned Wounded		150
Guns embarked		440
Vehicles embarked		15300
Ammunition		2,682,800
Ordinance Stores		921,300
Supplies etc.		2,207,300
Stores etc returned & discharged		743,200
	TOTAL	6,554,600 tons
Losses of Transports		11
	Hospital Ships	NIL
	Troops to France	5
Transport Sailings		8,330

From April 1916 to August 1918 the rescued crews of 45 ships numbering 954 men were brought into Newhaven Harbour.

These statistics were included in a letter entitled 'Supplies Shipped First War' sent to David Lloyd George in February 1920. The letter was a request for assistance in providing work for the Port following the end of the Great War. The lack of work was having a devastating effect on the local economy. See Appendix for a copy of the letter.

APPENDIX

1. ABBREVIATIONS/GLOSSARY OF TERMS

A. A.	Anti-Aircraft
A. I.	Adjustment Indicator – gun tide adjustment
A. S.C.	Army Service Corps
B.C. Post	Battery Command Post
Brs/Bdrs	Bombardiers
c. b.	Confined to Barracks
C. O.	Commanding Officer
C.S.M	Company Sergeant Major
C. Q.M.S.	Company Quarter Master Sergeant
Det.	Detachment, a group of men detached from their unit.
Grs/Gnrs	Gunners
Hydrophone	A microphone designed to be used underwater for recording or listening to underwater sound
L.B. & S.C.R	London, Brighton and South Coast Railway.
L. E. E.	London Electrical Engineers
Miniature Rifle	A rifle used for basic training in a bolt action rifle. It was introduced by the War Office as a result of poor British marksmanship in the Boer War.
O. C.	Officer Commanding
O. i/c	Officer in charge
O.C.R.E.	Officer Commanding Royal Engineers
O. R. Officers	Other Ranks, Privates and Non-Commissioned (N.C.O.s)
Piquet	Soldiers or troops placed on a line forward of a position to warn against an enemy advance, a picket in modern terminology.
Q. M.	Quarter Master
Inlying Picket	A detachment of troops held in camp or quarters, detailed to march if called upon.
L.B.S.C.R	London Brighton and South Coast Railway

M.G.	Machine Gun
M.G.C.	Machine Gun Corps
R. A.M.C.	Royal Army Medical Corps
R. E.	Royal Engineers
R. F.A.	Royal Field Artillery
R. G.A	Royal Garrison Artillery
Terrier Locomotive	L.B. & S.C.R. A1 Class 0-6-0T steam locomotives designed by William Stroudley. Built at the Brighton Works between 1872 and 1880. The class received several nicknames but affectionately known as 'Terriers' because of the distinctive bark of the exhaust beat.
T.F. or (T)	Territorial Force

2. BIBLIOGRAPHY

- Newhaven Fort Record Book 1902-1939, Army Book No. 360, in the National Archives reference WO 192/47.
- 'British Railways and the Great War', by Edwin A. Pratt, page 1033, London, Brighton and South Coast Railway, Newhaven Town Station - www.ournewhaven.org.uk.
- 'Remembrances of the Sussex R.G.A (Territorials)' – by Corporal Charles Edward Cornford, R.G.A. From the Fort Archives (Ref.: T8447)
- 'Wartime memories of Fort Newhaven' by Gunner John Williamson, R.G.A. From the Fort Archives (Ref.: T8442) – an article in 'Sussex Life' published in September 1982. Also, notes from Hilary Fogg (later Hobbs), granddaughter from interview with grandfather on 16th July 1978.
- 'Notes on the Newhaven Coastal Fort during 1914-1916' by a member of the 4th Company London Electrical Engineers from Newhaven Museum, Peter Bailey, supplied by Sqdn. Ldr. A. Akhurst from memoirs supplied by a relative of his.
- 'The Territorials 1908-1914' by Ray Westlake – Army Reforms introduced by Secretary of State for War Richard Haldane in 1907 with effect from 1st April 1908.
- Major A. J.Martineau, British Medical Journal 18 August, 1917 Casualties in the Medical Services page 233, also kingscollections.org/warmemorials/st-thomas-hospital/memorials/martineau-alfred-john.
- Major W F H Grinsted, Officers Service papers at the National Archives WO 74/29569.
- Major Dow, Officers Service Papers at the National Archives, WO 374/20493, the Private Papers of Dorothy Dow (daughter) held at the East Sussex Records office, The Keep, Brighton, ref. AMS6739.
- 'Royal Engineers Journal July-December 1913'
- 'The Long, Long Trail, The British Army in the Great War, Fortress Company R.E. and 50 A.A. Coy. www.1914-1918.net
- War Diaries of 578 Works Company (2/2 Sussex) File No. 116, Royal Engineers Museum, Gillingham
- Transcript from Historical Records, No.1 Depot R.G.A., Year 1914-15 by Major J.T. Chapman, R.A. Commanding Officer dated 20th May 1915.

- Western Front Assoc web site, the-british-generals-biographies, Brig. Gen. F G. Anley
- 'British Regiments, 1914-18' by Brig. E.A. James, O.B.E., T.D. – Royal Sussex Regiment p77, 1st (H.S.) Garrison Battalion the Buffs (East Kent) Regiment p45, 29th (Works) Battalion, Middlesex Regiment p94
- Diary of Major S.W.P. Beale, 4th Battalion, Royal Sussex Regiment in West Sussex Records office, Chichester ref. RSR/MSS/4/44
- Digest of Service of 3rd (Reserve) Battalion, Royal Sussex Regimen in West Sussex Records office, Chichester ref. RSR/MSS/3/34
- Second Lieutenant John Bolas Lane, Officer's Service Papers WO 339/33776, http://www.delvillewood.com/rolcallL.htm
- 'Newhaven in the Great War' – by G. D. Martineau, 3rd (Reserve) Battalion, Royal Sussex Regiment, The Sussex County Magazine date unknown, photocopy in Fort Archives.
- Bertrand Russell - Working Class Movement Library - http://www.wcml.org.uk/contents/protests-politics-and-campaigning-for-change/no-conscription-fellowship/; http://en.wikipedia.org/wiki/Clifford_Allen,_1st_Baron_Allen_of_Hurtwood
- 'Newhaven Fortress News' in West Sussex Records office, Chichester ref. RSR/MSS/4/59
- Imperial War Museum Documents, Pocket Diary for Capt. B. A. West ref. BAW/1/2 1 Jan to 31 Dec 1915
- East Sussex Records Office, The Keep, Brighton, Coroner's Reports

  Private Herbert Charles Jay, Ref. COR/3/2/1915/166
  Private Thomas Bartram, Ref. COR/1/3/220, ALSO British Army Service Records, National Archives WO 363; British Army Service Records 1760-1915 WO 97/2264 , 2265 Chelsea for Bartram and Barton, findmypast.co.uk
  Private Elias Luff, Ref. COR/1/3/303
  Private Cecil Clifton, Ref. COR/1/3/306
  Private Allen Bernard Sanders Ref. COR/1/3/446

- Lance Corporal Twine - East Sussex News 26th Jan 1917

Key to Source of Illustrations

Front Cover from Newhaven Fort Archives 2009

ESR	East Sussex Records Office
NAA	National Archives, Kew
NFA	Newhaven Fort Archives
NMM	Newhaven Maritime Museum
WSR	West Sussex Records Office

3. "NEWHAVEN DEFENCE SCHEME (PROVISIONAL) REVISED TO APRIL 1918"

NEWHAVEN DEFENCE SCHEME (PROVISIONAL)
REVISED TO APRIL 1918
(From Newhaven Fort Record Book, Army Book No. 360, held in National Archives WO 192/47 Part 1 Operation)

PREFACE
The attached DEFENCE SCHEDULE, in which the various factors are enunciated in detail, provides for the following MEASURES OF DEFENCE:

N.B. THICK FOG will be treated AS NIGHT.

1. NORMAL – THE MEASURES are ALWAYS IN FORCE BY DAY.

(a) NAVAL.

(I).	Port War Signal Station.	Watches all approach from the Sea.
(II).	Hydrophone Circle.	Indicates the approach of Submarines.

(b) MILITARY.

(I) GUNS in Fort can instantly be manned.
THE BATTERY has look-out men.

(II)	ROYAL DEFENCE CORPS.	Guards all Entrances to Newhaven Prohibited Area.
(III)	300 RIFLES WITH AMMUNITION,	stored at Transport Workers Battn., ready for issue.
(IV)	3rd ROYAL SUSSEX	available to man WESTERN Land Defences, O.C. Royal Sussex to command this Section.
(V)	TRANSPORT WORKER'S. BATTN	Ready to man EASTERN Land Defences within 20 minutes. O.C. Transport Worker's Battn., to command this Section.

BY NIGHT OR IN THICK FOG
The following ADDITIONS to the day measures are made:

(a) NAVAL

(I) Line of Trawlers anchored ½ mile off Shore, excepting in rough weather.

(b) MILITARY

(I)	PLATOON 3rd ROYAL SUSSEX	protects FORESHORE Eastern side of Harbour near Wireless Station & East Quay.
(II)	GUARD of N.C.O & 6 men 3rd ROYAL SUSSEX REGIMENT	Protect SEARCHLIGHTS on Breakwater
(III)	SEARCHLIGHTS on BREAKWATER	MANNED ready for INSTANT ACTION.

(IV)	2 MACHINE GUN TEAMS	sleep in Fort READY FOR ACTION on Foreshore, Western side of Harbour.

2. ALARM. (All troops in position in 20 minutes).

(I)	ALL UNITS	Stand to Arms.
(II)	TRANSPORT WORKER'S BATTN.	Armed.
(III)	TRANSPORT WORKER'S BATTN.	Send party of 1 OFFICER and 30 men to Foreshore on Eastern side of Harbour, and 4 parties of N.C.Oand 30 MEN EACH to hold 2nd LINE DEFENCES on Eastern Shore front.
(IV)	2 MACHINE GUNS (manned by 3rd Royal Sussex from Fort)	occupy Emplacements on Foreshore, WESTERN side of Harbour.

(V) IF ORDERS TO THAT EFFECT ARE ISSUED
Transport Worker's Battn., man Eastern Land Defences and 3rd Royal Sussex man Western Land Defences. Normally these two Battns. are in reserve.

NOTE
Support may be expected from Canadian Troops who will bring Machine Gun Batteries into position near the BUCKLE INN.

3. SPECIAL VIGILANCE.

Same as NORMAL, with the FOLLOWING ADDITIONS:
All Leave stopped.

BY NIGHT
(I) PLATOON from 3rd ROYAL SUSSEX proceeds to TIDE MILLS and finds posts on Foreshore, connecting up with Canadian post at BUCKLE INN.

(II)	NIGHT GUARD ON SEARCHLIGHT	Doubled
(III)	2 MACHINE GUNS (manned by 3rd Royal Sussex) FROM FORT	occupy Emplacements on Western Foreshore.

NOTE:- Canadian Troops will patrol the Coast East of BUCKLE INN.

4. GENERAL MOBILIZATION.

(I)	ARMY SERVICE CORPS.	Hand over sufficient Transport to 3rd Royal Sussex to render that Battalion MOBILE.
(II)	ARMY SERVICE CORPS	impress Transport for Station work from the CIVIL AUTHORITIES.
(III)	ROYAL ENGINEERS and WORKING PARTIES from 3rd ROYAL SUSSEX and from TRANSPORT WORKER'S BATTN.	Improve the EXISTING DEFENCES.

(IV) ALL SPARE RIFLES from 3rd Royal Sussex Regiment stored at Transport Worker's Battn., ready for issue to men of the Battalion.

GENERAL.

(I) ALL posts to be held – no retirement.

(II) Night dispositions will be taken up on the Foghorn sounding from the Breakwater.

(III) STATE OF ALARM IS TAKEN UP IN ANY OR ALL THESE NOTIFICATIONS:-

(a) Notification on telephone.

(b) Firing (Post that hears firing to notify Garrison Headquarters on 'phone)

(c) Alternate LONG and SHORT blasts on Hooter in Harbour
(d) "ALARM" sounded on Bugle (to be taken up by all Troops).

REMARKS

Although the Defence Scheme provides for meeting an attack of considerable strength with the defence force available it is thought that the present Garrison is not sufficiently strong to make a protracted defence.

It is presumed if an attack of considerable force was considered possible, the Garrison would be augmented.

In this case a new Defence Scheme would be prepared.

A. GENERAL

PORT OF NEWHAVEN

1. The Port of Newhaven is utilised at the present time as a Home Base for the Shipment of ammunition and supplies to the British Expeditionary Force, as a base for Naval Forces employed on escort duty for Government Transports and on mine sweeping and anti-submarine patrol duties and as a Seaplane Base [started in 1917] for submarine and Mine Patrol duties.

OBJECT OF GARRISON

2. The Garrison exists (a) for the defence of the Fort against hostile attack from the sea or land, (b) for defence within the limits of the Garrison Area against enemy landing forces with objectives beyond the Garrison (c) for the support of the Examination Service, the floating portion of which is under the Navy, and (d) for the protection of vulnerable points against acts of sabotage.

AREA OF GARRISON

3. The Area of the Garrison is bounded by the Coast Line from Friars Bay on the West to Blatchington Coast Guard Station on the East, and roughly by a circle of 1 ½ miles radius, having its centre at Newhaven Town Station.

(Pencil additions – 'This is roughly the outer boundaries of the parishes of PIDDINGHOE, TARRING NEVILLE, DENTON, DENTON-URBAN, SOUTH HEIGHTON and BISHOPSTONE.)

OBJECTS OF HOSTILE ATTACK

4. The probable object of hostile attack would be:-
   (a) to destroy the quays, shipping, ammunition and stores. A possible, though improbable object would be
   (b) to secure the harbour and beach for landing an invading force
   Pencil Addition (c) to block the harbour entrance.

FORMS OF ATTACK

5. The forms of attack considered likely and provided for are:-
   (a) Bombardment at night by enemy submarines.
   (b) A small landing party at night from enemy submarines.

Improbable forms of attack are:
   (c) A landing of considerable force preceded by a bombardment from the sea with the battery in the Fort as its objective.
   (d) An attack from the land by force which had already landed in the vicinity.

ATTACK BY HOSTILE AIRCRAFT

6. Attack by Hostile Aircraft is not provided for in this scheme, but forms the subject of separate orders. The Anti-Aircraft Defences are primarily responsible for repelling it and the orders for action by other Troops are subsidiary to the orders issued under this scheme.

SABOTAGE

7. The town of Newhaven within the Military Defences having been declared a Special Military Area under the Defence of the Realm Regulations, there is no reason to expect, subject to the efficiency of the control of persons entering the area, that acts of sabotage will be committed from within the Area.

PRINCIPLES OF DEFENCE

8. The general principles of the defence are:-

(a) Readiness under normal conditions to take prompt and energetic action to prevent a hostile landing by meeting the attack as soon as it arrives within the limits of effective fire, and

(b) Resistance to the last man on each line of defence, the first line being the foreshore itself.

B. FACTORS AFFECTING DEFENCE

COAST DEFENCES

9. The Harbour is protected by the Fort on the West side of the entrance, which is armed with two 6-inch B.L. Mark VII Guns. The Guns have a command of 140 feet above mean sea level and command the coast line and anchorage of Seaford Bay at a range of about 4000 yards and all the sea area east of a line drawn south 65 degrees west (true) to a range of 10,000 yards. The sea areas illuminated by two Defence Electric Lights, performing the double roles of Lighting and Observation Lights, sited in revolving turrets at the end of the Breakwater.

The area of fire of the guns and arcs of traverse of lights are shown on the attached 1-inch Ordnance Map (A) [not in possession]. Two Maxim Gun emplacements are sited below the Fort and command the mouth of the Harbour.

COAST ON WEST SIDE

10. West of the Harbour the cliffs are high and steep and no landing beyond the vicinity of the Breakwater is considered likely, though the cliffs might possibly be scaled at CHALK GAP near FRIARS BAY.

COAST ON EAST SIDE

11. East of the Harbour for 2 ½ miles in Seaford Bay the beach affords a good natural landing place. The 5 fathom line runs about 1000 yards from the shore. This beach is commanded by the guns of the fixed armament and as long as these remain in action it could not be used as a landing place by day.

EXTERNAL COMMUNICATIONS

12. The River Ouse divides the Garrison into two sections, Eastern and

Western and is crossed in Newhaven by a Swing Bridge, also by a Swing Bridge at Southease and by a Swing Railway Bridge at Southerham, near Lewes. It is navigable for small steamers to Lewes, min. depth 5 ft 6ins. The road and rail communications are clearly shown on the 1 inch Ordnance Map (A) [not found].

LAND DEFENCES

13. Wire entanglements and fences completely surround the town and harbour, also Denton Waterworks and South Heighton Cement Works, and are shown on Ordnance Maps (A) and (B) [not found]. Trenches constructed in August 1914 and still serviceable are also show. They extend in the Eastern Section for about ¾ mile northwards of the L.B.S.C.R. (Newhaven and Seaford Branch), and isolated Trenches exist on Rookery Hill to the east and at Denton. The ground from Friars Bay to Bollen's Bush in the Western section was formerly entrenched but holding these defences under the present scheme is not considered necessary. They are indicated in pale colour on the 6 inch Ordnance Map (B) [not found].

LOCATION OF TROOPS

14. The whole of the Combatant Troops permanently allotted to the Defence of the Garrison are located in the Western Section. This scheme depends upon the presence of other troops in the Eastern Section, and would require amendment if they were removed.

C. FORCE AVAILABLE FOR DEFENCE OF GARRISON

TROOPS ALLOTTED TO DEFENCE

15. The troops authorised for the defence of the Garrison consist of:

1 Special Reserve infantry battalion.
1 Company R.G.A. (T.F.).
1 Fortress Company R.E. (Electric Lights and Signals)
1 Works Company R.E. (T.F).

The other troops which are being used for the purpose of this Scheme are shown in para. 17.

ESTABLISHMENTS

16. The authorised establishments, armaments and locations are given in the table on page 160.

NOTES:

1. S.A.A.- Small Arms Ammunition
2. MLE – Magazine Lee-Enfield. A bolt-action, magazine-fed repeating rifle.
3. SM.L.E. - Short Magazine Lee-Enfield. Short refers to the length of the rifle.
4. E.Y. - Ernest Youlle, the inventor. It is an adaptation of the Lee Enfield rifle.
5. 1914 – 1914 Pattern Rifle (P14). Lee-Enfield with a 5 round magazine.
6. D.P. – Drill Purpose rifles. This is a rifle that has been altered so that it can no longer be fired. Used for rifle drill and weapon-handling tests.
7. The actual fighting strength of the infantry battalion varies within very wide limits. The remaining Units are kept up to establishment.

Unit	Officers	O.R. s	Guns	Ammo.	Lights	M/Guns	S.A.A	Rifles	S.A.A.	Location
3rd (Reserve) Btn. R.S.R.	40	1553	–	–	–	6 Lewis	*	500 S.M.L.E. for Drafts	**	Meeching Rise Camp
								730 1914 365 MLE 365 EY or DP		
2 Coy. Sussex R.G.A. (T.F.)	4	86	2 x 6 inch B.L. Mark VII	525 Rounds per Gun	–	2 Maxims manned by 3rd Btn. R.S.R.	*	86 1914	**	Fort
Fortress Coy. (Lights & Signals)	3	58	–	–	2 x 90 cm Projectors Clark Chapman Lamps	–		6 E.Y.	**	Fort
578 Works Coy. R.E.	3	147	–	–	–	–		18 MLE	**	Fort Hill Camp
Unit	Officers	Other Ranks	Guns	Ammo.	Lights	M/Guns	S.A.A.	Rifles	S.A.A.	Location
Total	50	1844	2	–	2	8	–	2070	–	

* 10,000 Rounds Equipment, 21,500 Rounds Reserve per Machine Gun

** 550 Rounds Equipment, 200 Rounds Reserve per Rifle.

OTHER TROOPS AVAILABLE

17. The following Troops are used, though not permanently authorised for the Defence of the Garrison:-

Unit	Officers	Other Ranks	Rifles	S.A.A.	Location	Normal Employment
1. Det of 102nd Protection Coy. Royal Defence Corps	3	100	126 Ross	40 Rounds per Rifle	On Outposts	Guards on Special Military Area & Vulnerable Points
2. Dets 12th & 13th Transport Workers Btns, Bedfordshire Regiment	10	400	Nil	Nil	Railway Road Camp	Transport Work in Harbour
TOTAL	13	500	126	–		

NAVAL FORCES

18. A variable number of Naval Ratings are present in the Port on board Torpedo Boats, Mine Sweepers, Drifters and Patrol Boats, and assistance would be rendered, if possible under the orders of the Senior Naval Officer, but no reliance can be placed on those forces as they would possibly be employed at sea when the emergency arose. Reliance is placed upon the Naval Authorities for Intelligence of the approach of hostile Submarines or other Vessels, which would be obtained from patrols or from a system of hydrophones which exists in the vicinity of the Port connected with a station at Cuckmere Haven.

AIR FORCES.

19. The personnel of the Air Station are also at times available with two Lewis Guns, but might be otherwise engaged.

ASSISTANCE FROM OUTSIDE.

20. The only troops located in the neighbourhood of the Garrison are the Canadian Training Centre at Seaford, and assistance in considerable force would be available provided other schemes for their movement elsewhere were not in force.

D. COMMUNICATIONS

O. i/c ARMY SIGNALS.

21. The O.C. Fortress Coy. , R.E. acts as O. i/c Army Signals who will act as the technical adviser of the Garrison Commander, and be responsible to him for the organisation and employment of the inter-communication service. The Post Office is responsible, under the general supervision of the O. i/c Army Signals, for maintenance of all lines except Defence Electric Light lines, and for the working of the Post Office Exchange.

TELEPHONES.

22. The system of Telephone communications is shown on Diagram (C) [not found].

COMMUNICATION WITH COMMAND HEADQUARTERS.

23. Under normal conditions, Garrison Headquarters are in communication

with Eastern Command Headquarters through the public telephone exchange system, or through the direct Anti-Aircraft Warning Line to Home Forces.

During Special Vigilance a direct telephone circuit will be provided from Eastern Command Headquarters to Garrison Headquarters, also a direct Telegraph circuit from Eastern Command Headquarters to Newhaven Post Office.

INTERCOMMUNICATION WITH NAVY.

24. Communication with the Senior Naval Officer is effected either through the public telephone exchange or by Defence Line to the Battery Commander's Post, and verbal transmission thence to the Port War Signal Station, which adjoins it, and is connected by a speaking tube. The Senior Naval Officer is in direct communication with the Port War Signal Station, and also with the Admiralty. The Port War Signal Station is connected by the Coast Communication Line with all Coast Guard Stations between Hove and Beachy Head.

EMBARKATION COMMANDANT.

25. Communication with the Embarkation Commandant is through the public telephone exchange.

UNITS AND OUTPOSTS.

26. Garrison Headquarters are connected by direct circuits with the Military Exchange in the Fort Guard Room, from which direct circuits lead to the Battery Commander's Post, and certain Units and Outposts. Other Units are connected only to the Post Office Telephone Exchange.

POWER STATION.

27. The Battery Commander's Post is connected by direct telephone circuit with the Power Station where the Harbour Lights are controlled and a Hooter can be sounded to convey an alarm to the Harbour. The Embarkation Commandant is also connected with the Power Station.

DESPATCH RIDERS

28. Four Motor Cyclist Despatch Riders are attached to the Garrison.

E. ALLOTMENTS OF DEFENCES TO UNITS

COY. R.G.A.

29. The 2/Coy. Sussex R.G.A. mans the fixed Coast Defence Armament and will also undertake the immediate defence of the Fort. The Battery commander will further be responsible for the tactical handling of the defences of the Breakwater and foreshore below the Fort.

FORTRESS COY. R.E.

30. The Fortress Coy. , R.E. (Electric Light Section) mans the Defence Electric Lights, under the tactical control of the Battery Commander, and has no other responsibilities. The Signal Section is responsible for telephone communications and despatch riders.

WORKS COY. R.E.

31. The Works Coy. , R.E. is held in reserve for any R.E. Services that the situation may require.

SPECIAL RESERVE INFANTRY BATTALION

32. The 3rd Battalion Royal Sussex Regiment is responsible for the first line of defence on the foreshore in both Eastern and Western Sections. For this purpose it maintains a Guard of 2 N.C.O. s and 6 men in the BREAKWATER AREA by day and night, two Maxim Gun detachments in the FORT by night, ready to take post in the BREAKWATER AREA at short notice, and a Piquet (sic) of 1 officer and 20 other ranks near the NAVAL WIRELESS STATION in the Eastern Section.

(In times of special Vigilance the Maxim Gun detachments and the Piquet remain at their posts by day and night, and the Piquet is reinforced by 1 Lewis Gun and detachment and by 16 other ranks to provide two Sentry groups at TIDE MILLS and near the BUCKLE INN respectively, and a Patrol between these points.)

The bulk of the Battalion acts as the General Reserve under the Garrison Commander.

A Coast Watching outpost at CHALK GAP near FRIARS BAY is furnished on emergency.

TRANSPORT WORKERS

33. The Detachments Transport Workers Battalion of the Bedfordshire Regiment will, so long as rifles are available, be responsible in an emergency for the second line of defence in the Eastern Section. This extends from the South end of the EAST WHARF to the salient in the existing trenches of the Eastern Defences, immediately north of the L.B. & S.C.R. (Newhaven and Seaford Branch).

The Detachment will also form a local Reserve in the Eastern Section under the Garrison Commander. Half of this Reserve can be used by the O.C., Detachment, (who will act as Commander, Eastern Section, in emergency) at his discretion.

A Guard on the L.B. & S.C.R. Pumping Station and Reservoir at DENTON will also be furnished in emergency.

300 Stands of Arms (1914 pattern rifles), 50 rounds of S.A.A. [small arms ammunition] per rifle in bandoliers, and 50 rounds per rifle in boxes, on the charge of the 3rd Royal Sussex Regiment, are kept in the RAILWAY ROAD CAMP, for issue to the Detachment on the alarm being given.

No defence duties are allotted to this Detachment except when the emergency has actually arisen, and work on the quays is suspended.

ROYAL DEFENCE CORPS

34. The Royal Defence Corps have no duties allotted to them beyond furnishing permanent guards on the following Vulnerable Points:-
    (i) Harbour Area ("North Quay" and "Wireless" Sections).
    (ii) Trench Warfare Supply Depot, South Heighton Cement Works.
    (iii) Glynde Reach Railway Bridge.
    (iv) Southerham Railway Bridge.

And Examining Guards at the following entrances to the Newhaven Special Military Area:-
    (i) Town Station.
    (ii) Seaford Road.
    (iii) Lewes Road.
    (iv) Brighton Road.

F. METHOD OF MEETING HOSTILE ATTACK

(a) Bombardment at Night from Submarine

INFORMATION

35. Information as to the presence of Hostile Submarines and their position will probably be obtained from Hydrophones or from other naval sources and will be communicated by the Senior Naval Officer to the Garrison Commander and Battery Commander through the Port War Signal Station.

ACTION BY COAST DEFENCE GUNS & LIGHTS

36. Action will in the first instance be taken by Naval Forces, but on receipt of this warning the Battery will be manned ready to engage and the Defence Electric Lights held ready to expose as soon as the enemy is located within the radius of effective action. This radius is approximately 3,000 yards from the Defence Electric Lights in the sector covered by both lights and 2,000 yards in the Sectors covered only by one light, but will vary with atmospheric conditions and will be left to the discretion of the Battery Commander.

ACTION BY OTHER UNITS

37. Whenever possible other units will be warned by telephone to "Stand to for bombardment" but the first intimation will probably be the commencement of the Bombardment. Officers will remain with the Troops, ready to turn out and take cover in the event of their area being shelled.

POSITIONS FOR UNITS

38. The following positions will be taken up by Units when necessary:-
    (i) 3rd Btn. Royal Sussex Regiment.
    line HILL BARN – WORKHOUSE – CHURCH HILL
    (ii) Royal Defence Corps A.S.C. and other details in Fort Glacis Camp [in military engineering glacis is an artificial slope of earth used in late European Fortresses so constructed as to keep any potential assailant under the fire of the defenders until the last possible moment]

Passages in Fort

(iii) 578th Works Coy. R.E.
Practice Trenches behind FORT HILL CAMP.

(iv) Dets. T.W. The Bedfordshire Regiment.
Trenches behind RAILWAY ROAD CAMP.

COMMUNICATIONS WITH GARRISON HEADQUARTERS & FIRE PIQUETS

39. Telephonic communication with Garrison Headquarters will be maintained by all Units from their Orderly Rooms and Fire Piquets will remain in the vicinity of hutments.

(b) Night Landing Party from Submarines

INFORMATION & IMMEDIATE ACTION

40. Information of the attempt to land a small party from Submarines would probably be received from the Senior Naval Officer, through reports from Patrols and Hydrophones, but in the event of the enemy succeeding in approaching the Harbour unobserved, the first intimation might be received from the Sentries on the foreshore and Breakwater, in which case the Piquet at NAVAL WIRELESS STATION and the BREAKWATER GUARD will at once attack the enemy without waiting for orders, prevent him from landing, or pin him to the beach. It is impressed on all ranks concerned that no retirement from this first line of defence is to take place.

TRANSMISSION OF INFORMATION & ALARM

41. Information of the attempt at landing will be immediately telephoned to Garrison Headquarters. The Piquet at the NAVAL WIRELESS STATION will make use of the telephone to the PORT WAR SIGNAL STATION for this purpose. The Battery Commander, if he has reason to believe a landing is taking place, will at once telephone to the POWER STATION and order the Hooter to be sounded in long and short blasts, and will also order the "Alarm" to be sounded outside the FORT GATE. The "Alarm" will be taken up by other Units in the Garrison and action immediately taken on the standing orders. The Transport Workers Battalion will also be warned by telephone by Garrison Headquarters.

ACTION BY BATTERY COMMANDER.

42. The Battery will be manned and Defence Electric Lights exposed with a view to locating and opening fire on hostile craft. On no account will the Defence Electric Lights be traversed north of the BUCKLE INN without special orders from the Garrison Commander as such action might imperil the defence on the foreshore and assist the enemy; but a Sentry beam will be kept trained as far as possible, on the BUCKLE INN and the light elevated and depressed so as to illuminate the surface of the water on this line, and assist the defence on the foreshore in locating the enemy. The Maxim Gun detachments, if not already in position will be ordered to take post, and will come under the tactical control of the Battery Commander.

3rd BATTALION ROYAL SUSSEX REGIMENT.

43. The Battalion will immediately be issued with 150 rounds of S.A.A. per man and will fall in on Meeching Rise, ready to move under the orders of the Garrison Commander. A Piquet of 2 N.C.O. s and 16 men will be despatched to CHALK GAP, FRIARS BAY, to prevent attempts to scale the cliff at that point.

TRANSPORT WORKERS

44. Rifles and Ammunition will be issued to all men in Camp and to men who will return to Camp from the quays at the double on hearing the Alarm. The O.C. Detachment will assume the duties of Commander, Eastern Section. Four parties made up to 30 men each will move off as quickly as possible to the following posts on the second line of defence which they will reach in 20 minutes, and from which no retirement is on any account to take place:-
    (i) Along the Eastern Trenches as far as the salient immediately north of the L.B. & S.C.R. (Newhaven & Seaford Branch)
    (ii) By RAILWAY ROAD, F.F. (?) and L.B. & S.C.R. as far as junction of NEWHAVEN and SEAFORD BRANCH with trenches.
    (iii) By RAILWAY ROAD & F.F across HILL CROSS by F.B. and by F.F. as far as sheds on sidings near the shore.
    (iv) Along EAST WHARF as far as it's South end.

The remainder of the Detachment for which rifles are available, (i.e. 180 O.R.), will form a local Reserve for the Eastern Section, under the Garrison Commander. The O.C. Detachment may draw upon this Reserve up to 90 O.R. for counter-attack or whatever object he considers necessary, without reference to Garrison Headquarters, but the remaining 90 will not be moved except with the permission of the Garrison Commander.

R.E. WORKS COY.

45. The 578th (Sussex) Works Coy., R.E. will remain with their transport at Fort Hill Camp for employment wherever required under the O.C.R.E.

OTHER UNITS

46. All other units will await orders at their respective Headquarters. All motor cyclists Despatch Riders will report at Garrison Headquarters.

(c) landing in Considerable Force

or

(d) Attack from the Land

47. In view of the small number of troops available for Defence, and the fact that a landing in force on this part of the Coast is improbable under conditions existing at the time of preparation of this Defence Scheme, no special provision is made for Defence against these forms of attack, and the disposition of available forces is left to be decided on in accordance with whatever situation may arise.

*****

NOTE: The original document in the National Archives show some manual additions/amendments in pencil. The majority of which are indecipherable. Where clearly legible they have been included.

4. DAILY STRENGTH RETURN NEWHAVEN GARRISON 13TH APRIL 1917

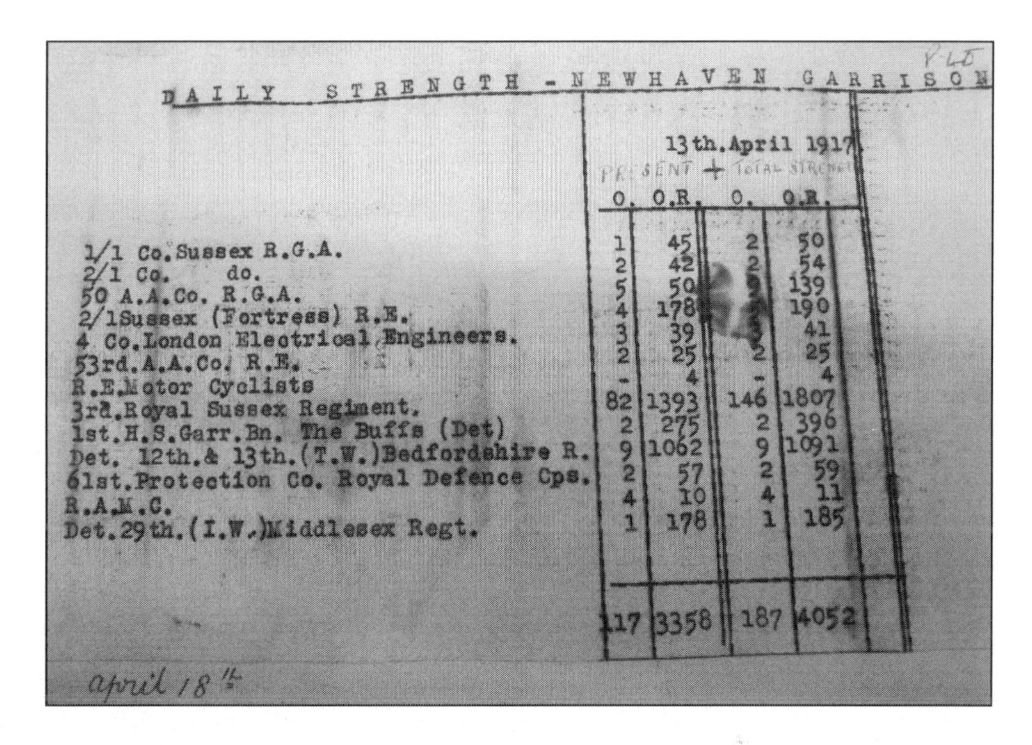

P.40

DAILY STRENGTH - NEWHAVEN GARRISON

13th. April 1917.

PRESENT + TOTAL STRENGTH

	O.	O.R.	O.	O.R.
1/1 Co. Sussex R.G.A.	1	45	2	50
2/1 Co. do.	2	42	2	54
50 A.A.Co. R.G.A.	5	50	[illegible]	139
2/1Sussex (Fortress) R.E.	4	178	[illegible]	190
4 Co.London Electrical Engineers.	3	39	3	41
53rd.A.A.Co. R.E.	2	25	2	25
R.E.Motor Cyclists	-	4	-	4
3rd.Royal Sussex Regiment.	82	1393	146	1807
1st.H.S.Garr.Bn. The Buffs (Det)	2	275	2	396
Det. 12th.& 13th.(T.W.)Bedfordshire R.	9	1062	9	1091
61st.Protection Co. Royal Defence Cps.	2	57	2	59
R.A.M.C.	4	10	4	11
Det.29th.(I.W.)Middlesex Regt.	1	178	1	185
	117	3358	187	4052

april 18th

5. NEWSPAPER REPORT ON SUSSEX (FORTRESS) R.E. ANNUAL DINNER 7TH JAN 1916

of Mr. Woods to undertake the office, and no doubt they would hear further about the scheme after he had interviewed the officials at the Central Office for the county and obtained further details as to the scheme.

SUSSEX (FORTRESS) ROYAL ENGINEERS.

NEW YEAR'S DINNER AT NEWHAVEN.

The second annual New Year's dinner of the 2/1st Sussex (Fortress) Royal Engineers was held at the Church Room, Newhaven, on Tuesday evening, and proved an unqualified success. Seldom, if ever, has the room been more effectively decorated, and depended from the rafters were some grotesque-looking Chinese lanterns. This work was carried out by Sapper P. A. Sutton, assisted by Sappers Hardy, Saunders and Tasker.

A bountiful repast had been excellently prepared by the regimental cook (Corporal Bunkle), and it was expeditiously served by the following ladies: Mrs. Wells, Mrs. Bunkle, Mrs. Dickinson, the Misses Balkham and Bunkle, of Seaford; and the Misses M. Bennett, Cantell, Parsons, Seal, Simmons, M. Richardson and R. Richardson, of Newhaven. Mr. W. Coleman, of Seaford, was the carver.

C.S.M. Wells, C.Q.M.S. Orford, Sergts. Chinchin and Coleman, Corpls. Hoad and Stentiford, Lance-Corpl. R. Bennett and Sappers P. Bennett, Cooke, Peckham and Sutton, who formed the committee, and in whose capable hands was left all the arrangements for the dinner, are to be congratulated that everything went off so smoothly and without a hitch.

Capt. F. C. Sanders (officer commanding 2/1st Sussex F.R.E.) presided, and was supported by Lieuts. W. S. Gorringe and W. Young, and Mr. R. Garrett (Royal Naval Division). C.S.M. Wells, supported by the members of the committee, occupied the vice-chair, and others present were as follows:—

2nd Corpl. Arnold, Sapper Atkinson.

2nd Corpl. Arnold, Sapper Atkinson.
Sergt. Balkham, Lance-Corpl. Bennett, Lance-Corpl. F. Burgess, Sappers A. W. Bellairs, I. A. Booth, R. G. Bosworth, W. Buckwell, P. Bennett, E. Burgess, E. Burton, A. H. Bacon, P. J. Batchelor, Barfoot and Bartholomew, Driver Bolton.
Corpl. Christmas, Sappers C. F. Cole, J. J. Coleman, H. C. Cole, W. Cole, W. P. Cottington, Carey, A. Cooke and F. C. Cole.
Sappers J. Divall and C. Darter.
2nd Corpl. Elliott, Sappers A. Elliott and B. Elliott, Driver G. Eager.
Sappers J. F. French, H. Funnell, H. R. Fears, A. Holberton, Hayler, T. Forster, T. C. Finch, A. E. Frise, G. Funnell and C. Fiest, Driver W. Freeman.
Lance-Corpl. Gander, Sapper A. Gibbs, Driver M B. E. Garrett, Bugler Green.
Sappers W. Hardy, Hedger, T. Hills, W. G. Hilton, S. Hubble and W. Hammond, Drivers A. V. Harvey, T. F. Holter and F. Hughes.
Sappers S. James, D. W. M. James, C. T. Jupp and W. Jutton.
Sapper P. F. J. Knight, Driver G. Keeley.
Lance-Corpl. Law, Sappers F. Levett, J. Leister and T. Lewis, Driver A. V. Lovegrove.
Lance-Corpls. Mercer and Morling, Sappers C.

Matthews, F. J. Miller, A. Mason and G. W. Moon.
Sapper Nice.
2nd Corpl. Orford.
Sergt. Pullen, Sappers H. Peacock, W. Page, H. S. Pulling, C. Peckham, C. Pelling, E. Pursglove, Pegler, H. Parsons, W. A. Palmer, H. J. Payne, A. C. P. Parks, J. Paris, T. Peckham and T. J. Parks, Driver W. Parsons.
Sappers S. G. Rawlings, Ranger and A. J. Richardson, Driver A. Richardson.
Lance-Corpl. Sherwin, Sappers H. Sanders, J. M. Scott, H. Stevens, W. Styles, T. Saull, L. Seymour, A. H. Streeter, H. Simmons, P. A. Sutton and W. R. Stoner, Bugler Satchell.
Sappers H. E. Turner, W. H. Turner, W. J. Truman, S. Terry, G. Towner, E. W. Tyler, A. J. Tasker, V. Taylor, J. D. Taylor and F. C. Tupper.
Sappers L. Venus, B. Vaughan and T. Venus.
Sappers R. G. Weller, F. C. Williams, Wren and J. T. Walder.
Driver H. Young and Mr. W. J. Mills (late "B" Co. 1st Sussex R.E. Volunteers).

Capt. C. E. Whelan (O.C. Administrative Centre, Seaford) wrote regretting his inability to attend and wishing the company a very enjoyable time. A similar communication was also received from the staff at Seaford Centre. Justice having been done to the good things provided, Lieut. YOUNG submitted "The King," which was enthusiastically honoured.

Lieut. GORRINGE, in the course of an excellent speech, submitted "The Navy and Army."

Sergt. BALKHAM, on rising to respond, received a great ovation. He remarked that the Navy and Army were both engaged in the greatest conflict the world had ever known—and he hoped ever would know—and it behoved every man to do his bit, no matter whether it be officer or man. They must get themselves fit and ready for anything which might crop up, for when they were in the thick of the fight advancing or retreating by night and digging oneself in and keeping out of sight in the day, it caused a great strain on the nerves. They (the Sussex Fortress R.E.) had a lot to do yet to get themselves fit, so they must buck up and let the little trifling matters they had at times pass the same as the Navy their watch. With Navy and Army pulling the same way and pulling together it would not be long before they wound up the "Watch on the Rhine" and brought the war to a glorious and successful ending (applause).

Mr. GARRETT, in proposing "Success to the 2/1st Sussex Fortress R.E.," wished them a very prosperous New Year.

Capt. SANDERS, in response, thanked Mr. Garrett for his good wishes. Although it was the second annual dinner of the Sussex Fortress Royal Engineers which they were celebrating, it was really the first one of their particular Company, for, as all were aware, their Company had only been formed a few months—in October last. The facilities for training were very much improved since they left Seaford. They had excellent equipment and stores, and he hoped that after the holiday they would settle down to hard training and in a few months be ready if necessary to go to France (applause), and carry out any duty the Government might give them to do (applause).

C.S.M. WELLS supported the previous speaker's remarks, and spoke in felicitous terms of his connection with the Company and also with the Company which was serving in France. Perhaps they might say he had a leaning towards the Company across in France because he had a son in it. Perhaps he had, but he knew that both No. 1 Company and No. 2 Company were equally prepared to do their duty to their uttermost (applause).

Sergt. CHINCHIN proposed "The Ladies," and said it was very kind of them to give up their time as they had done to come and wait on them (applause).

Mrs. WELLS suitably responded, and said they were only too pleased to come and do their little bit.

Towards the close of the evening Capt. SANDERS said that in the stress of business he had forgotten to refer to the excellent arrangements made by the cook (Corpl. Bunkle). He had always served them well, not only on such occasions as these, but every day they had occasion to appreciate his most excellent cooking (applause).

Sapper P. Bennett presided at the piano, and also gave several excellent songs. Others contributing to the harmony were Corpl. Christmas, Sapper Sutton, Corpl. Stentiford, Sergt. Chinchin, Sapper W. H. Turner, Sergt. Coleman, C.Q.M.S. Orford and Sapper H. C. Cole.

Rank	Surname	First Name(s)/ Initials	Comment
Captain	Sanders	F.C.	Commanding Officer. Gave speech.
Lieutenant	Gorringe	W.S	Gave a speech
Lieutenant	Young	W.S	Gave Toast 'The King'
C.Q.M.S.	Orford		Committee/Arrangements. Sang
C.S.M.	Wells		Gave speech
Sergeant	Balkham		Gave speech, response to Lt. Gorringe
Sergeant	Chinchin		Com./Arrgmts.Toast 'The Ladies'.Sang.
Sergeant	Coleman		Committee/Arrangements. Sang.
Sergeant	Pullen		
Corporal	Bunkle		Regimental Cook. Cooked meal.
Corporal	Christmas		Sang.
Corporal	Hoad		Committee/Arrangements
Corporal	Stentiford		Committee/Arrangements. Sang.
2nd Corporal	Arnold		
2nd Corporal	Elliott		
2nd Corporal	Orford		
L/ Corporal	Bennett	R.	Committee/Arrangements
L/Corporal	Burgess	F.	
L/Corporal.	Gander		
L/Corporal.	Law		
L/Corporal.	Mercer		
L/Corporal.	Morling		
L/Corporal.	Sherwin		
Driver	Bolton		
Driver	Eager	G.	

Rank	Surname	First Name(s)/ Initials	Comment
Driver	Freeman	W.	
Driver	Garrett	M.B.E.	
Driver	Harvey	A.V.	
Driver	Holter	T.F.	
Driver	Hughes	F.	
Driver	Keeley	G.	
Driver	Lovegrove	A.V.	
Driver	Parsons	W.	
Driver	Richardson	A.	
Driver	Young		
Sapper	Sutton	P.A.	Decorated Room
Sapper	Hardy		Decorated Room
Sapper	Saunders		Decorated Room
Sapper	Tasker		Decorated Room
Sapper	Bennett	P.A.	Committee/Arrangements
Sapper	Cooke		Committee/Arrangements
Sapper	Peckham		Committee/Arrangements
Sapper	Sutton		Committee/Arrangements
Sapper	Atkinson		
Sapper	Bellairs	A.W.	
Sapper	Booth	I.A.	
Sapper	Bosworth	R.G.	
Sapper	Buckwell	W.	
Sapper	Bennett	P.	Played piano and sang.
Sapper	Burgess	E.	
Sapper	Burton	E.	
Sapper	Bacon	A.H.	
Sapper	Batchelor	P.J.	
Sapper	Barfoot		
Sapper	Bartholomew		
Sapper	Cole	C.F.	
Sapper	Coleman	J.J.	

Rank	Surname	First Name(s)/ Initials	Comment
Sapper	Cole	H.C.	Sang.
Sapper	Cole	W.	
Sapper	Cottington	W.P.	
Sapper	Carey		
Sapper	Cooke	A.	
Sapper	Cole	F.C.	
Sapper	Divall	J.	
Sapper	Darter	C.	
Sapper	Elliott	A.	
Sapper	Elliott	B.	
Sapper	French	J.F.	
Sapper	Funnell	H.	
Sapper	Fears	H.R.	
Sapper	Holberton	A.	
Sapper	Hayler		
Sapper	Forster	T.	
Sapper	Finch	T.C.	
Sapper	Frise	A.E.	
Sapper	Funnell	G.	
Sapper	Fiest	C.	
Sapper	Gibbs	A.	
Sapper	Hardy	W.	
Sapper	Hedger		
Sapper	Hills	T.	
Sapper	Hilton	W.G.	
Sapper	Hubble	S.	
Sapper	Hammond	W.	
Sapper	James	S.	
Sapper	James	D.W.M.	
Sapper	Jupp	C.T.	
Sapper	Jutton	W.	
Sapper	Knight	P.F.J	

Rank	Surname	First Name(s)/ Initials	Comment
Sapper	Levett	F.	
Sapper	Leister	J.	
Sapper	Lewis	T.	
Sapper	Matthews	C.	
Sapper	Miller	F.J.	
Sapper	Mason	A.	
Sapper	Moon	G.W.	
Sapper	Nice		
Sapper	Page	W.	
Sapper	Pulling	H.S.	
Sapper	Peckham	C.	
Sapper	Pelling	C.	
Sapper	Pursglove	E.	
Sapper	Pegler		
Sapper	Parsons	H.	
Sapper	Palmer	W.A.	
Sapper	Payne	H.J.	
Sapper	Parks	A.C.P.	
Sapper	Paris	J.	
Sapper	Peacock	H.	
Sapper	Peckham	T.	
Sapper	Parks	T.J.	
Sapper	Rawlings	S.G.	
Sapper	Ranger		
Sapper	Richardson	A.J.	
Sapper	Sanders	H	
Sapper	Scott	J.M.	
Sapper	Stevens	H.	
Sapper	Styles	W.	
Sapper	Saull	T.	
Sapper	Seymour	L.	
Sapper	Streeter	A.H.	

Rank	Surname	First Name(s)/ Initials	Comment
Sapper	Simmons	H.	
Sapper	Sutton	P.A.	Sang.
Sapper	Stoner	W.R.	
Sapper	Turner	H.E.	
Sapper	Turner	W.H.	Sang.
Sapper	Truman	W.J.	
Sapper	Terry	S.	
Sapper	Towner	G.	
Sapper	Tyler	E.W.	
Sapper	Tasker	A.J.	
Sapper	Taylor	V.	
Sapper	Taylor	J.D.	
Sapper	Tupper	F.C.	
Sapper	Venus	L.	
Sapper	Vaughan	B.	
Sapper	Venus	T.	
Sapper	Walder	J.T.	
Sapper	Weller	R.G.	
Sapper	Williams	F.C.	
Sapper	Wren		
Bugler	Green		
Bugler	Satchell		

6. CARTOON AND POEM - 'KING GEORGE'S BOYS AT NEWHAVEN 1914'

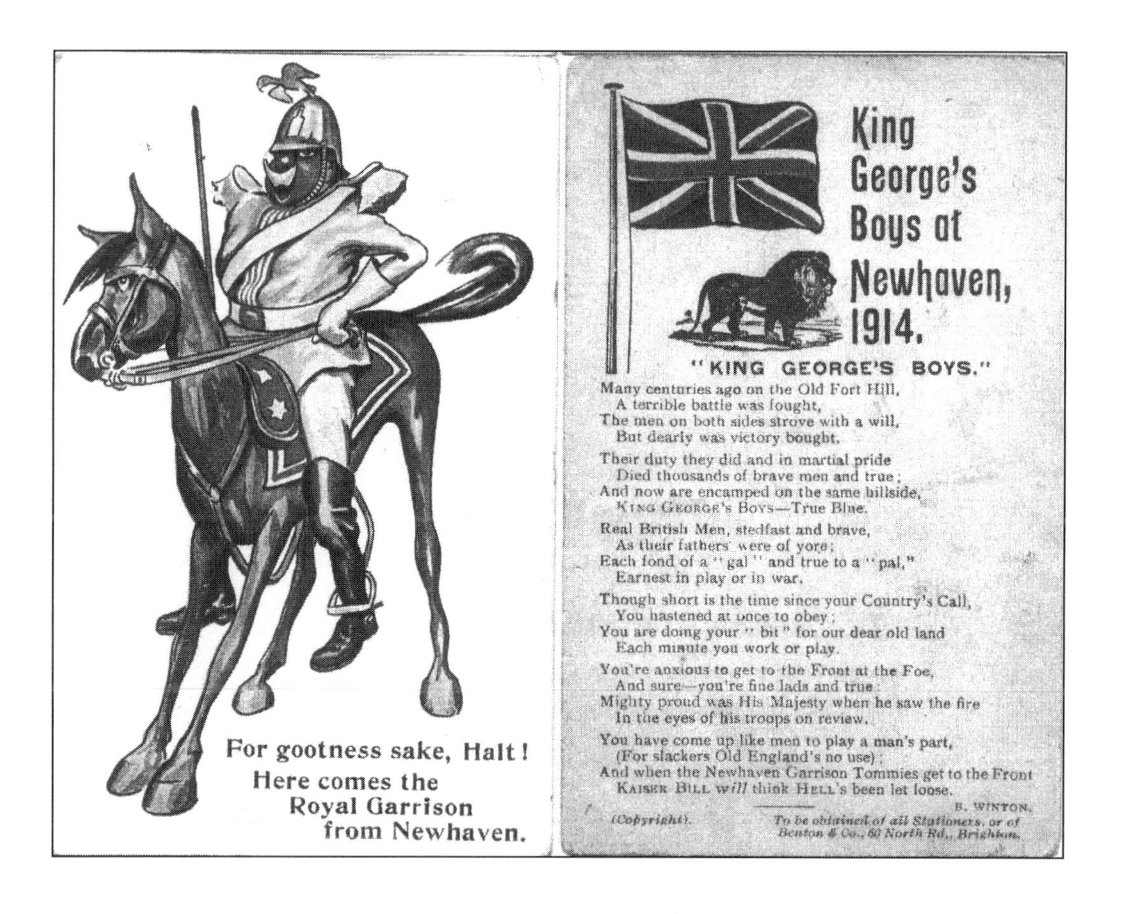

King George's Boys at Newhaven, 1914.

"KING GEORGE'S BOYS."

Many centuries ago on the Old Fort Hill,
A terrible battle was fought,
The men on both sides strove with a will,
But dearly was victory bought.

Their duty they did and in martial pride
Died thousands of brave men and true;
And now are encamped on the same hillside,
KING GEORGE'S BOYS—True Blue.

Real British Men, stedfast and brave,
As their fathers were of yore;
Each fond of a "gal" and true to a "pal,"
Earnest in play or in war.

Though short is the time since your Country's Call,
You hastened at once to obey;
You are doing your "bit" for our dear old land
Each minute you work or play.

You're anxious to get to the Front at the Foe,
And sure—you're fine lads and true:
Mighty proud was His Majesty when he saw the fire
In the eyes of his troops on review.

You have come up like men to play a man's part,
(For slackers Old England's no use);
And when the Newhaven Garrison Tommies get to the Front
KAISER BILL *will* think HELL's been let loose.

B. WINTON.

(Copyright). *To be obtained of all Stationers, or of Benton & Co., 60 North Rd., Brighton.*

7. THE ARMAMENT IN THE FORT IN THE GREAT WAR

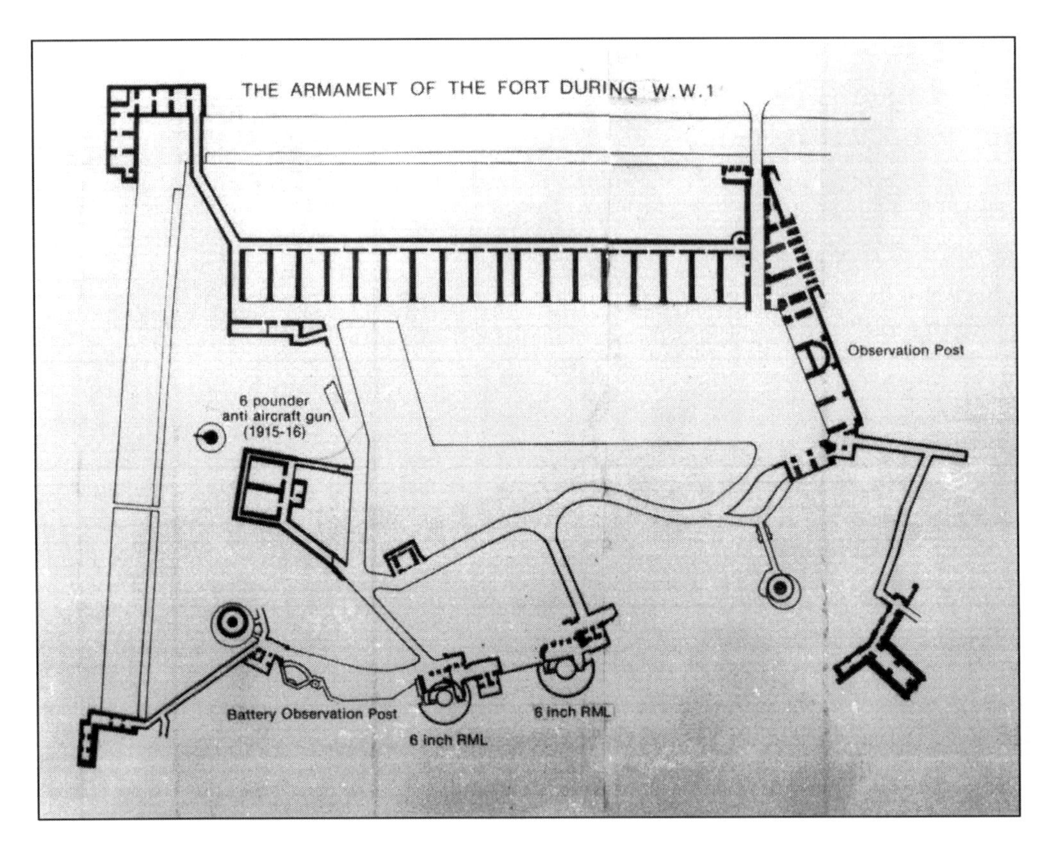

The Armament of the Fort in the Great War [NMM]
Note: the 6 inch guns were "BL" (Breach Loading) not "RML" (Muzzle Loading).

8. LETTER TO DAVID LLOYD GEORGE FEBRUARY 1920

REF. SUPPLIES SHIPPED - FIRST WAR.

"A SECOND & CLEAR COPY OF A LETTER SENT TO THE RIGHT HONOURABLE DAVID LLOYD GEORGE.

DATED FEBRUARY 1920.

SIR. WE THE UNDERSIGNED INHABITANTS & WORKERS OF THE PORT OF NEWHAVEN RESPECTFULLY & URGENTLY ASK YOUR ASSISTANCE IN HELPING US TO PROCURE MORE SHIPPING FOR THE PORT OF NEWHAVEN.

THE WHOLE EXISTENCE OF THE TOWN & PORT DEPEND UPON THE AMOUNT OF SHIPPING CALLING HERE.

AT THE PRESENT TIME SCORES OF FAMILIES ARE BEING BROUGHT TO THE VERGE OF STARVATION THROUGH THE ABSENCE OF COAST-WISE SHIPPING.

DURING THE WAR NEWHAVEN RENDERED INVALUABLE SERVICE TO THE CALL MADE UPON IT, & EMPLOYED AT DIFFERENT TIMES SOME 2,700 CIVILIAN LABOURERS, IN ADDITION TO WOMEN WORKERS FROM LEWES, BRIGHTON, PIDDINGHOE, SEAFORD, SOUTH HEIGHTON & OTHER PLACES, & THE LABOUR COMPANY.

TODAY THE PORT EMPLOYS ON AN AVERAGE SOME 25 TO 40 CASUAL LABOURERS PER DAY, THIS NUMBER BEING ONLY EXCEEDED WHEN COAL BOATS ARE IN THE HARBOUR.

NEWHAVEN IS A MOST FAVOURABLY SITUATED PORT, AND IS CAPABLE OF GREAT DEVELOPMENT.

SEAFORD BAY COULD BE MADE INTO ONE OF THE FINEST SHELTERED BAYS UPON THE SOUTH COAST OF ENGLAND. THE PORT ITSELF COULD BE IMPROVED AND ADDITIONAL WET DOCKS CREATED, ALSO DRY DOCKS. THERE ARE GREAT POSSIBILITIES IN THE DISTRICT FOR THE OPENING AND DEVELOPMENT OF FACTORIES, POSSESSING AS IT DOES ALREADY, DIRECT RAIL COMMUNICATION WITH LONDON & OTHER PLACES.

DURING THE WAR THE HARBOUR WAS USED IN THE NATIONAL INTEREST, AND WE NOW URGE THAT THE PORT SHOULD BE USED TO RELIEVE THE SERIOUS CONGESTION ASSOCIATED WITH OTHER PORTS. SHIPS UP TO 2,000 TONS CAN BE WORKED AT NEWHAVEN FOR EITHER COAL OR GENERAL CARGO.

DURING THE LATE WAR THE FOLLOWING SHIPS & STORES WERE DISPATCHED WITHOUT A SINGLE HITCH.

FROM AUGUST 14TH 1914 TO NOVEMBER 11TH 1919

TROOPS EMBARKED — OFFICERS ——— 104
" " — MEN ——— 9,504
9608

RETURNED WOUNDED. ——— 150
GUNS EMBARKED ——— 440
VEHICLES EMBARKED ——— 15,300

AMMUNITION — TONS ——— 2.682.800
ORDNANCE STORES ——— 921.300
SUPPLIES .ETC. ——— 2.207.300
STORES.ETC. RETURNED & DISCHARGED. TONS ——— 743.200
TONS 6.554.600

LOSSES OF TRANSPORTS ——— 11
" " HOSPITAL SHIPS ——— NIL
" " TROOPS TO FRANCE ——— 5
TRANSPORT SAILINGS ——— 8330

APRIL 1916 TO AUGUST 1918. THE RESCUED CREWS OF 45 SHIPS NUMBERING 954 MEN WERE BROUGHT INTO NEWHAVEN HARBOUR.

9. NEWHAVEN FORT SITE PLAN 2014

Key

1. Guard Room, Shop, Exit
2. Theatre
3. The Fort Collection
4. The Fort & Newhaven
5. Life in the Fort
6. School Room
7. Sussex Land, Sea & Air
8. Sussex & Surrey Yeomanry
9. ROC – Nuclear Defence
10. ROC – World War Two
11. Dieppe & D-Day
12. The Home Front
13. Romney Hut
14. Fire Point
15. Searchlight Café
16. World War One
17. Newhaven Fort Amateur Radio Group

SITE PLAN

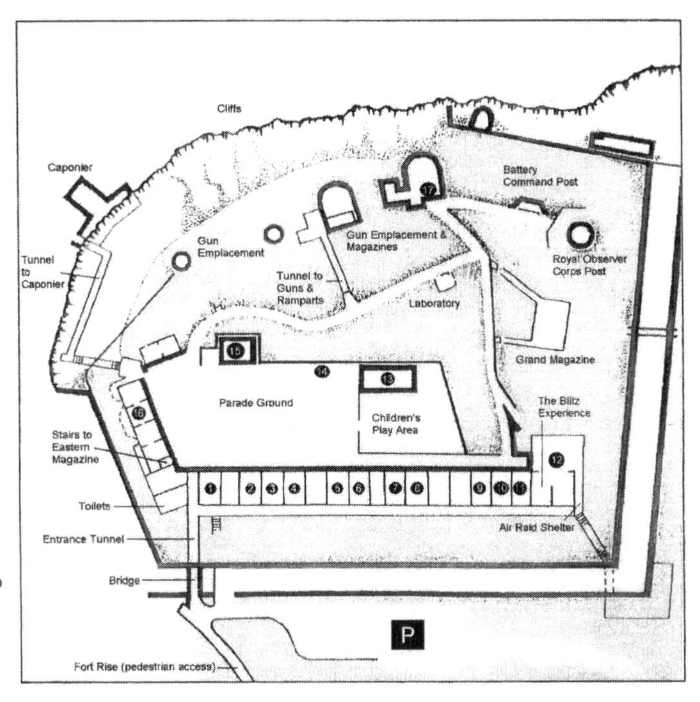

10. ACKNOWLEDGEMENTS

I would like to thank Lewes Disttrict Council for their help and support and particularly the kind and supportive staff at Newhaven Fort for their interest and assistance during the production of this book and their contribution by imparting their knowledge of the Fort and the Newhaven area. Simon Cochran, the manager, Philip Baldock, the curator, Ed Tyhurst, who's knowledge of the Fort and its history is second to none, Kath Dudley and Steve Watkins.

I am grateful to local Newhaven historian and former manager of the Fort for many years, Ian Everest, for reviewing a draft copy of the book. It was important to check for any local historical inaccuracies in the book and Ian's expert knowledge was ideal for achieving this. Also, to another Newhaven historian, Jenny Flood for providing information about Newhaven servicemen.

Many thanks to Mike Cornford for his kind permission to include the account by his uncle Charles Edward Cornford of his experiences whilst stationed in the Fort with the Sussex Royal Garrison Artillery during the Great War. It really was extremely useful and important information.

I wish to record my thanks to the East Sussex Records Office, The Keep, Brighton, the West Sussex Records Office, Chichester, the Royal Engineers Museum, Gillingham and the Newhaven Maritime Museum for their helpful staff and for their permission to include photos and material from their archives. Also, to the staff at the National Archives which was an invaluable source of information about the Fort and men who served in Newhaven.

My thanks to John Harrap for providing me with information about his great-grandfather Major J. G. Chapman and No. 1 Depot, Royal Garrison Artillery during its time in Newhaven.

Last but not least, warm thanks to my wife, Sue, for enduring my 'away days' researching the information and the, at times, frequent, seemingly endless sessions in front of my pc.

INDEX

53rd Welsh Division 94
Anley, F.G., Brig.Gen. 60, 64
Army Service Corps 155
Bishopstone 64-66, 80, 98-99, 157
  Buckle Inn 22, 154-155, 165, 169
Blatchington Coastguard Station 15, 80, 156
Border Regiment 99, 104
Brighton 18, 27, 30, 32, 38, 45-47, 54, 97, 99, 128, 138
Cambridge 92, 94-95, 105
Chalk Gap 22, 158, 165, 169
Chichester 75, 96, 105, 130
Croydon 72
Cuckmere Haven 23, 163
Denton 19, 23, 64-66, 76, 80, 93-94, 98, 157, 159, 166
Dover 18, 67-68, 70, 96, 129-130, 133
Eastbourne 97, 100
  Beachy Head 164
Edmund Loder, Sir 92
Friars Bay 15, 22, 156, 158-159, 165, 169
Galt, H.M., Dr. 143, 146
Glynde Reach 70, 166
Gosport 68, 100, 129
Hampshire Regiment 96, 100
Horsham 75, 79, 82-84, 86, 89, 91-94
Hove 45, 143, 146, 164
Hythe 87-88, 92
Kitchener, Lord 100
L.B.S.C.R. 22, 159, 166, 169
Lewes 46, 81, 90, 97, 159
Lloyd George, David 147, 183
Mill Hill 73
Montgomery, Capt., R.G.A. 143
Naval Forces 12, 13, 20, 23, 63, 152-3, 156, 163-5, 167-8
  Pascoe, Capt., R.N. 34
Newhaven
  Beaty's Barn 19
  Bollen's Bush 159
  Breakwater 12, 21-22, 36, 42, 53-55, 76, 98, 153, 155, 158, 165, 168
  Bridge Hotel 18
  Bridge Street 59, 61, 118
  Brighton Road 70, 89, 93, 166
  Chapel Street 19, 116, 118, 132, 139
  Christ Church 100
  Church Hill 167
  Cinema - Chapel Street 19
  Cinema - High Street 19
  Conservative Club 89
  Drill Hall 18-19, 78, 82
  Foreshore 21, 153-155, 158, 165, 168-9
  Garrison H.Q. 63
  Gibbon Road 27
  Gymnasium 19, 27, 30, 87, 128
  Harbour 7, 13, 15, 22, 34-36, 55, 70, 72, 74, 76, 87, 98, 147, 153-154, 156-159, 162, 164, 166, 168
  Harbour Railway Station 20, 82
  Hill Barn 79-80, 167
  Isolated Area 76-77, 79, 81
  Isolation Hospital 19
  Lewes Road 70, 89, 166
  Liberal Club 19
  Marshall Hall 18
  Meeching Farm 19
  Meeching Rise 20, 96, 169
  Meeching Rise Camp 24, 70, 96, 102
  Military Hospital 116, 133, 138, 143
  Mill Creek 77
  Moneybag Hill 27

Naval Wireless Station 22, 153, 165, 168
Newhaven Gas & Coke Co. 30
Old Brewery 19
Port 12-13, 18, 20, 23, 34, 98, 147, 152, 156, 163-164, 167-168, 183
Railway Road Camp 23, 26, 72, 88, 166, 168
Railway Train - 'Lousy Lou' 97
Recreation Ground, Fort Road 30, 77, 80, 91, 95-96, 101, 103
River Walk 19
Seaford Road 70, 166
Seaplane Base 12, 156
Sheffield Hotel 27, 30
Station Road School 78, 85
Swing Bridge 26, 76, 159
Tidemills 12, 22-23, 154, 165
Town Railway Station 15, 20, 70, 94, 98-99, 115, 143, 156, 166
West Beach 43
Workhouse 19, 80, 88, 93, 167
Norfolk Regiment 100
Norton 19, 80, 98, 99
Piddinghoe 64-66, 99, 157
Poverty Bottom 76, 80
Price, P., Capt., R.F.A. 143-145
R.A.M.C. 19, 27, 46, 116-117, 128
Cathcart, E.P., Capt. 116, 146
Gilkes, Lt. 116, 132-133, 135
Hill Shaw, R., Capt. 40, 116
Johnson, F., Cpl. 116, 140
Moulson, Major 116
Paley, F.J., Lt.Col. 128
West, B.A., Capt. 116-117
Will, Lt. 116, 138, 140
River Ouse 12, 26, 71, 158
Rottingdean 93
Royal Defence Corps 22, 70, 71, 153, 162, 166, 167
Royal Engineers - Fortress Company 50-51
Royal Engineers - Lights and Signals 12, 21, 25, 50-51, 53-59, 158-159, 161, 163, 165, 167, 169
Levin, A.E., Major 53, 104
Vitty, T.H., Capt 53, 104, 118
Royal Engineers-Sussex Fortress 12, 50, 59-62, 118
2/1st Sussex Coy. R.E.
Balkham, Sgt. 176
Bennett, P.A., Spr. 177
Bennett, P., Spr. 177
Bennett, R., L/Cpl. 176
Bunkle, Cpl. 176
Chinchin, Sgt. 176
Christmas, Cpl. 176
Cole, H.C., Spr. 178
Coleman, Sgt. 176
Cooke, Spr. 177
Gorringe, W.S., Lt. 176
Hall , L.H., Spr 57
Hardy, Spr. 177
Hoad, Cpl. 176
Kenyon, A.W., Lt. 61
Orford, C.Q.M.S. 176
Peckham, Spr. 177
Philcox, H.H., Spr 48
Sanders, F.C., Capt. 60, 176
Sanders, P.R., Capt. 118
Saunders, Spr. 177
Stentiford, Cpl. 176
Sutton, Spr. 177
Sutton, P.A., Spr. 177, 180

Tasker, Spr. 177
Tucknott, A.V., Spr 59
Turner, W.H., Spr. 180
Tyler, E.W., Spr 52
Warren, H.G., Lt. 61
Wells, C.S.M. 61, 176
Young, W.S., Lt. 176
578 Works Company 25, 60-62, 159, 161, 168, 170
Royal Garrison Artillery - No. 1 Depot 12, 20, 27-28, 33, 67-69, 124
Batty, Bdr. 124
Bigwood, Sgt 124
Brew, G.M., Lt. 68, 124
Brown, Cpl. 124
Chapman, J.T., Major 67-69
Church, G.R.M- Lt.Col. 63, 67
Couchman, Gnr. 124
Evans, Sgt 124
Greenhall, Cornet Cpl. 124
Gurr, Bdr. 124
Hosford, D.A., Capt 67-68
Hurst, Bdr. 124
Mayne, R.C., 2nd Lt. 68, 118
Parminter, Sgt. 124
Pearson, Gnr. 124
Quire, Bdr. 124
Robinson, Sgt. 124
Roddis, Sgt 124
Smith, Sgt. 124
Vaux, C.A., Capt. 68, 124
Vickers, Bdr. 124
Whyte, T.A., Capt. 67
Royal Garrison Artillery - Sussex (T.F.) 12, 18, 20-21, 24, 27-47, 54, 58, 104, 118, 159, 161, 165
1 Company 18
2 Company 21, 24, 31, 38, 161, 165
Balcombe, W.H., Bdr. 58
Beaumont, Lt. 40
Cornford, C.E., Cpl. 27-39, 45-46, 55
Cornford, C.G., Batt.Sgt.Maj. 29, 31, 41
Cornford, W.H., Act.Sgt.Maj. 38
Dow, W.A., Major 40, 46-47, 104, 113
Greenhall, Cpl. 33
Grinsted, W.F.H., Capt. 40, 45-46, 104, 118
Jones, G.J., 2nd Lt. 40
Larking, Master Gnr. 32, 39
Lyons, T., Trumpt.Maj. 27, 33
Martineau, A.J.M., Major 40, 45-46, 104
Montgomery, J.E., 2nd Lt. 40
Payne, R., Cook 34
Roberts, K.G., Lt. 40
Thunder , R.W.V., 2nd Lt. 40
Wallis, J., Sgt.Maj. 38
Williamson, J.W., Gnr. 30-32, 35-39
Royal Sussex Regiment
2nd Battalion 64, 82, 96, 104, 129, 138
3rd Battalion 21, 23-25, 63-64, 70-71, 96-115, 128-146, 153-155, 165-167, 169
Allen, R.C., Pte. 113-115
Apperley, W.H.W., Capt. 100
Appleyard, W., Major 104
Ashworth, Capt. 97
Barnard, H., Sgt. 138
Barrett, R., L/Cpl. 142
Bartlett, Cpl. 134
Bartram, T., Pte 129-136

Beckett, E., Pte 134
Beynon, L.St.P., Capt. 104
Boniface, R.S.M. 97
Boyne, L.L., Capt. 104
Carver, H, Pte. 101-102
Church, R., Capt. 96
Clayton, Lt. 132, 135
Clifton, C., Pte. 139-140
Dean, C.G., Pte. 141
Elliott, T., Sgt. 133
Goring, F.Y., Lt. 141-142
Hankey, C.A., Lt.Col. 47, 63-66, 96-97, 104, 113
Jay, H.C., Pte 128
Lane, J.B., 2nd Lt. 104-112
Lloyd, A.W.K., Capt. 104
Luff, E., L/Cpl. 138-139
Maidlow, F., Pte 140
Martineau, G.D., Lt. 70-71, 96-100
Naldrett, J., Sgt. 133-134
Parkin, A.J., Capt 104
Peacham, J.A., C.S.M. 141-142
Plews, E., Pte. 143
Sanders, A.B., Pte. 143-146
Short, Sgt. 97
Soal , A., Cpl. 139
St. Croix, C.de., Capt 104
Twine, A.T., L/Cpl. 140-142
Watson, A., L/Cpl. 134-135

4th Battalion 12, 20-21, 75-95, 118
Beale, S.W.P., Major 75-76, 84-85, 88, 94-95
Bennett , E.W., Capt. 82-83, 86
Beris, Col. 76
Borrer, J.M., 2nd Lt. 82-83, 86
Butler, A.W., 2nd Lt. 92
Campbell, C., Lt. 79, 83
Campbell, C.H., Lt. 77, 79, 83
Campbell, E.R., Lt. 85-86, 89
Campion, W.R., Lt.Col. 81, 84-85, 92
Churcher, Sgt. 82
Churcher, E.C., 2nd Lt. 82, 90
Clarke, E.S., 2nd Lt. 80, 86-89
Constable, B., Capt. 86, 88, 91
Constable, G., Capt. 86, 89, 91
Corden, Q.M.S. 83
Cullen, C.S. 83
Duffield Jones, Capt. 81, 85-86, 89, 93, 118
Frank, R.J.B., Lt. 79, 81, 85-86, 88
Godman, C.R.B., Capt. 76, 86, 88, 91
Goring, F., 2nd Lt. 83-84, 88, 93
Gray, H.T.S., Capt. 85-86, 88, 90, 93
Hankey, Lt. 76, 84
Helme, R.M., Lt.Col. 84
Hodgson , E.T., Capt. 82-84, 86
Hook, Sgt.Maj. 80
Jebb, 2nd Lt. 86-89
Kenderdine, W.H., Lt. 79, 83
Loder, J., 2nd Lt. 83, 87-88, 90
Loder , R.E., Lt. 85, 87-88
Maples, Lt. 79, 83
Matthews, H.E., Capt 79
Messel, H.G., Lt. 83-84, 88, 93
Middleton, R.C.S., 2nd Lt. 83, 85, 88
Mostyn, E.H., Capt. 78, 81, 85-86, 88, 92
Mostyn, E.H.J.D., Lt.Col. 75, 91-92, 94
Reid, S.K., Lt. 78, 85, 87-89,
Ridley, 2nd Lt. 81, 86, 89, 92
Spring, Sgt. 79

St George, C.F.L., 2nd Lt. 82, 84, 88, 92
Stone, Sgt 79
Weekes, A.N.H., Capt. 83, 85-86, 88
Weekes, C.R.H., 2nd Lt. 78, 83, 85-86, 88-89
Wraight, W.F., Lt. 82
Wright, J., A/Sgt.Maj 80
Wyatt, Cpl. 81
9th Battalion 92
Russell, Bertrand 113, 115
Seaford 23, 36, 59-60, 64, 79-80, 94, 97, 99-100
Canadian Training Centre 23, 100, 154-155, 163
Seaford Bay 12, 158
Sherrard, L.A., Major R.E. 104
Shoreham 79-80, 100
South Heighton 20, 70, 98, 159, 166
Cement Works 64-66, 157
Southease 93, 159
Southerham 70-71, 159, 166
Southwell, Henry, Archdeacon of Lewes 77, 81, 90
Tarring Neville 65-66, 157
Telscombe Cliffs 97
Thetford 73
Transport Workers Battalion 22, 72, 153-155, 168-170
12th & 13th Btn., Beds. Reg. 22, 72, 162, 166, 168
Wadington, Major, South Eastern Coast Defence 18
Young, J.C., Maj.Gen., Home Counties Division 78